THE
CHINESE
STORYTELLER'S
BOOK

THE
CHINESE
STORYTELLER'S
BOOK
Supernatural Tales

MICHAEL DAVID KWAN

TUTTLE PUBLISHING
BOSTON • RUTLAND, VT • TOKYO

This edition published in 2002 by Tuttle Publishing, an imprint of Periplus Editions (HK) Ltd., with editorial offices at 153 Milk Street, Boston, Massachusetts, 02109.

Library of Congress Cataloging-in-Publication Data

Kwan, Michael David, 1934-2001-
    The Chinese storyteller's book : supernatural tales / by Michael David Kwan.
    p.cm.
    ISBN 0-8048-3418-0 (pbk.)
    1. Folklore--China. 2. Tales--China. I. Title.

GR335 .K94 2001
398.2'0951--dc21   2001037005

Distributed by

North America, Latin America, Europe
Tuttle Publishing
Distribution Center
Airport Industrial Park
364 Innovation Drive
North Clarendon, VT 05759-9436
Tel: (802) 773-8930
Toll free tel: (800) 526-2778
Fax: (802) 773-6993
Toll free fax: (800) 329-8885

Japan
Tuttle Publishing
RK Building, 2nd Floor
2-13-10 Shimo-Meguro,
Meguro-Ku
Tokyo 153 0064
Tel: (03) 5437 0171
Fax: (03) 5437 0755

Asia Pacific
Berkeley Books LTD
130 Joo Seng Road
#06-01/03
Olivine Building
Singapore 368357
Tel: (65) 280-1330
Fax: (65) 280-6290

06 05 04 03 02   9 8 7 6 5 4 3 2 1
Printed in the United States of America

CONTENTS

FOR KIRIN,
MY SPECIAL MUSE

THE FOX FAERY'S
WEDDING

*I*n the center of the town where I grew up, there used to be a
deserted mansion. The place had been abandoned so many years
ago that no one remembers the people who once lived there. By day
curious passersby would sometimes peep through the cracks of the
moldy wooden gate, but nobody ventured near after dark, for the
house was said to be inhabited by Fox Faeries.

Magistrate Yinn, who became quite famous as the arbiter of right
and wrong in the Emperor's court, came from the same town. We
attended the Academy together, and a merry bunch we were, spending
more time in taverns than at our books.

I remember it was a month or two before the Imperial
Examinations. A group of us gathered at a tavern near the abandoned
mansion to calm our pre-examination jitters. Yinn was in high spirits. He was one of those irritating people who excels without any
apparent effort. I was quite the opposite and frankly jealous of his
confidence. As the afternoon faded into dusk, those who had to

make their way home past the haunted mansion were anxious to leave, for Fox Faeries might be abroad.

"Fox Faeries!" scoffed Yinn, rolling his eyes eloquently. "What rubbish! And coming from educated, sophisticated young men!"

That remark caused a great hubbub.

"There are Fox Faeries!" I cried before I could stop myself.

"What is a Fox Faery?" Yinn rounded on me with laughter in his eyes.

I summoned up all the old wives' tales I'd ever heard.

"Why they are very old foxes . . ."

"How old?" Yinn was already the stickler for detail that would make his name in later life.

"Hundreds of years old . . ." I countered.

"How can a fox live that long?" mused Yinn.

"By living in harmony with its environment . . ." I said trying not to sound lame. Though the others were silent I sensed their amusement at my discomfiture. Yinn called for another jar of wine. When it arrived he filled our cups before returning to the debate on Fox Faeries.

"If I live in harmony with my environment," said Yinn with a gesture that encompassed the room, "I would be a faery too. In the pickled state one becomes larger than life, therefore, supernatural!"

The others crowed with laughter.

"It's not that simple," I plunged on. "The ancient fox acquires wisdom and the gods permit it to take on human form between dusk and daybreak . . ."

"But to what purpose?" Yinn pursued straight-faced.

"It's a test to see if the fox is worthy of evolving into a human . . ."

"Something like the Imperial Examinations!" someone gibed. Everybody laughed.

"Fox Faeries bewitch people," I cried, hot under the collar, "and they become creatures of the night too!"

Yinn laughed in my face.

"Since you don't believe there are Fox Faeries," I shouted, "spend the night in the haunted mansion and I will buy you a feast like you've never tasted before."

It was a mean-spirited wager, for we all knew Yinn was poor and struggled to keep up with the rest of us. Yinn looked at the gloating faces around him. Those who had been laughing with him a moment earlier had switched sides. He deliberately downed another cup of wine, wiped his mouth on his sleeve, and replied, "I accept."

The group grew somber. Another crock of wine helped calm our quiverings. It was completely dark when Yinn threw his cloak around his shoulders and swaggered in the direction of the haunted mansion. The rest of us followed at a safe distance to make sure he went in. When we saw him climb over the wall, we retreated to the tavern to wait for dawn.

I shall do my best to tell the story as I heard it from Yinn years ago.

A sliver of moon filled the garden with strange shadows. Small unseen creatures scurried among the underbrush. Ghostly brambles plucked at him out of the dark as Yinn picked his way toward the mansion along a cobbled footpath slick with moss. The door gave with a shriek of rusty hinges, rousing a swarm of bats that flapped noisily about him for an instant. Then there was silence so thick you could cut it with a knife. The mansion was festooned with cobwebs and reeked with decay. Yinn groped his way up a rickety staircase to a terrace overlooking the garden that had gone to seed. He found a spot that was clear of debris, wrapped himself in his cloak, and with a brick for a pillow, settled down for the night. Although he was determined to stay awake, the wine he had imbibed began to work on him. Lulled by the wind murmurs in the trees, Yinn soon fell asleep.

Hours later Yinn was wakened by the barking of foxes. One at first, answered by many others from far and near. Then he heard the sound of movement hurrying toward the house. In a moment footsteps not unlike his own sounded in the rooms below. Laughter and voices filtered up the staircase, though he could not catch the words. Yinn broke into a cold sweat. At that moment he wished he hadn't accepted the wager to spend the night in this wretched house. For that matter, he wished he was anywhere but where he was.

Footsteps were coming up the stairs. Yinn huddled deeper into the folds of his cloak. Through slitted eyes he watched the top of the stairs. A young man dressed like a servant appeared, holding high a lamp, turning it this way and that peering into the gloom. Yinn caught a glimpse of a narrow, sharp-featured face crowned with sleek black hair done in a knot at the top of the head. The long, slanted eyes glowed yellow in the lamplight. The nostrils flared as he sniffed the air. The lips pulled back revealing sharp white teeth and the curiously pointed ears convinced Yinn this was no ordinary being. An old man with an imposing mane of silver white hair and a long flowing beard followed.

"What seems to be the matter, Steward?" the old man inquired in a cultivated voice.

The servant raised his lamp and surveyed the terrace one more time. "There!" he hissed pointing in Yinn's direction. The old man peered after him.

"It's only a human," he said equably. "Hold the lamp closer so I can see him more clearly."

The Steward approached gingerly and raised the lamp so that the light fell upon Yinn's face. The old man studied it, brows furrowed in thought. The old man had the gentle air of a scholar about him. Whereas his Steward had a cunning, almost mean look.

"Let me get rid of him, Master!" the Steward hissed.

"The human will not harm us," the old man replied in the same gentle tone. "Let us get on with our business."

The Steward started to protest, but the old man motioned him to be silent.

"Our guests will be arriving soon and there is work to do," he reminded the Steward. Seeing the other's crestfallen look, he relented a little. "Have one of the pageboys watch him, but he mustn't be disturbed," he said. "I'm to be notified the moment he wakens."

Yinn screwed his eyes tight shut. His body ached in every muscle, but he gritted his teeth and forced himself to be still, convinced as long as the Fox Faeries believed he was asleep he would be safe.

The air was suddenly filled with the barking of foxes. Hundreds of them seemed to be converging upon the mansion. As suddenly as it started, the barking stopped. In a moment footsteps were scurrying past him mingled with the murmur of conversation and laughter. Music sounded somewhere in the house. Finally, the tantalizing aroma of food overcame fear. Yinn opened his eyes.

He found himself on a terrace of gleaming white marble. Splendid red lacquered pillars supported a finely carved ceiling, under a roof of pale green tiles that glowed in the moonlight. In the garden, wonderfully gnarled pines leaned darkly over beds of moss. Red and white carp swam lazily in the pond. Night-blooming flowers scented the air. This must be the way it used to be, thought Yinn. He was so engrossed that he did not notice the pageboy ordered to watch him, running off to report his waking.

A voice beside him startled Yinn out of his reverie. After introducing himself as Master Hu—a surname that has the same sound as the word for "fox"—the old man, wreathed in smiles, added, "Kind sir, you must join my guests. It is my daughter's wedding, and a mortal among us on such an occasion is a good omen."

Yinn glanced through the open doors of the great hall, at the brocades, silks, and jewels of the guests assembled within.

"I couldn't . . ." he stammered, more self-conscious of his disheveled appearance than afraid.

The old man seemed to read his mind, for he would not be put off.

An elegant lady, slightly younger than the old man, emerged from the hall as they spoke.

"Ah! Here is my wife," said the old man by way of introduction. "Perhaps she can persuade you to join us."

The lady beamed. Her fathomless black eyes seemed to reach into his soul, and Yinn's resistance melted. She took his arm and drew him gently to the high table set at the far end of the great hall.

"You shall sit in the place of honor," she insisted.

The table was set with the finest porcelains and ivory, and spread with a dazzling array of food. Yinn thought of the fox's usual diet and shuddered. However, his hostess pressed such delicate tidbits upon him that he soon forgot his qualms. Once he was used to them, Yinn decided he had never been in better company. His fellow guests were not only elegantly turned out but highly intelligent. Indeed, their witty and wide-ranging conversation was worthy of the most fashionable salons in the town. Furthermore, he was accepted as an equal. Yinn forgot his companions were creatures of the night and began to enjoy himself.

A fanfare sounded outside. The guests rose as a body, craning their necks at the door. The old man beamed with pleasure as a handsome youth came striding across the room with all the assurance and grace of a young fox. After they had exchanged salutations, the old man drew the bridegroom to the seat beside Yinn.

"Come, my boy," he said. "Entertain our guest of honor, till the bride arrives."

More food and wine was served. All the niceties of a wedding feast were observed.

Presently, the old man leaned toward his wife and in a whisper loud enough to be overheard inquired, "Is it not time?"

"It is, my Lord," she twinkled and, turning, whispered instructions to her maid. As the servant left the room, laughter stopped and conversations broke off in mid-sentence. A hush of anticipation fell upon the room.

"What's happening?" inquired Yinn.

The bridegroom had risen to his feet, flushed and eager.

"My bride is coming," he breathed.

The door to an adjoining room was flung wide. She was small, delicately formed, robed in red silk that enveloped her like a sheath of flame when she moved. The bridegroom bounded across the room to take her hand. A wave of applause swept the hall as the handsome young couple made their way slowly among their well-wishers, exchanging pleasantries. Yinn's heart hammered painfully against his ribs for she was the most exquisite maiden he had ever seen. Indeed, she was his ideal of feminine beauty and grace come to life. He couldn't keep his eyes off her. He almost swooned with joy when she came to sit beside him. He seemed to drown in her eyes, to be privy to her thoughts. The rest of the room faded away. Nothing existed for Yinn except this beautiful young girl. He was only vaguely aware of the old man ordering the Steward to fetch the gold goblets for a toast.

The Bride filled the goblets from a matching beaker.

"This is a very special wine," she said, offering Yinn the first goblet.

"Saved many years for just such an occasion," added her father.

It was a heady, full-bodied vintage with a subtle bouquet that coiled warmly through him. The joy of the new couple filled him with a nameless longing. The room took on the haze of a dream that he wanted to go on and on. With a pang he realized that the bride and groom were leaving and his ideal of beauty and grace would be lost forever. He downed the last of the wine. The goblet that she had handed him was the only tangible evidence of this night. He resolved to keep it as a remembrance of the exquisite girl who had captured his heart.

The other guests were taking their leave. As his host and hostess busied themselves seeing them out, Yinn slumped across the table pretending to be overcome by drink, but stealthily tucking the goblet into the voluminous sleeve of his robe.

The hall was soon empty except for the old couple and the Steward directing the servants cleaning up.

"Everything we borrowed must be returned to their proper owners," the old man reminded his Steward as he sank into a chair at the far end of the room to talk quietly with his spouse.

"My Lord, our guest of honor has fallen asleep!" Yinn heard his hostess remark to her husband.

"It's just as well," murmured the old man with an almost perceptible note of regret in his voice. "If he remembers anything of this night, I hope it will be as a pleasant dream . . ."

A heated exchange between the Steward and one of the servants cut him short.

"Is something wrong?" asked the old man.

"One of the gold goblets is missing!" cried the servant.

The old man rose to his feet.

"That's impossible," he said to the Steward. "It must have been misplaced. Look again."

"We've searched the house . . ." countered the Steward.

"Search again . . ."

"But it's almost daybreak!" cried the Steward.

"Then waste no time . . ." The old man's tone brooked no argument.

The servants scattered through the house. Yinn remained slumped across the table , forcing himself to breathe evenly, watching the others from behind his eyelashes. In the distance a cock crowed. The old man tilted his head toward the sound. Otherwise, he showed no signs of agitation. His wife traced a fingertip across her cheek, and moistened her lips nervously with the tip of her tongue. The old man laid a comforting hand on her shoulder.

"Don't worry. They'll find it."

But they did not.

The cock crowed again.

The servants clustered fearfully at the door of the room, gibbering at one another.

The Steward's eyes narrowed as they settled on Yinn.

"Master, the human must have taken it!" he cried. His voice had become guttural, and he seemed to have difficulty forming words. "Let . . . me . . . search . . . him!"

"No!" The timbre of the old man's voice had also changed. "The human must not be disturbed!"

The Steward's nostrils quivered impatiently.

"Master, I . . . smell it . . . on him," he insisted.

"Perhaps he is right," the old man's wife murmured through the handkerchief she held to her face. "You mustn't hesitate, my Lord! It grows light!"

The cock crowed again.

"Please, Master! Before . . . it's . . . too . . . late," growled the Steward. His features were slowly reverting to those of a fox. The old man looked at Yinn long and hard.

"My friend wouldn't steal," he asserted.

"He's not your friend," wailed his wife, "he's a human and humans are greedy!"

Doubt clouded the old man's face. Twice Yinn felt the old man standing over him, as if about to wake him, and then, sighing deeply, moved away.

"The goblet is lost," he sighed, "but only for a while. It will be returned to its rightful owner when the time comes."

Outside the sky was turning light. One by one the servants, the Steward, and even their mistress were turning into foxes. As the first streaks of sunlight touched the mansion, the old man's features melted into that of a gray fox that disappeared down the stairs. Yinn kept still a moment longer. When he was sure he was alone he picked himself up. The great hall was heaped with rubble where the roof had caved in. The terrace was littered with broken tiles and the garden choked with weeds. Not a trace of the glittering festivities of the night before remained.

That was Yinn's story when he joined us at the tavern.

"Fox Faery's wedding, indeed!" I sneered, out of sorts, after a wretched night worrying while Yinn was having the time of his life. I was not a gracious loser. "Let's see the goblet."

From the folds of his cloak Yinn produced a small gold goblet, the likes of which I had never seen before or since. When I finally found my tongue, I croaked rather lamely, "It's the most beautiful goblet I've ever seen."

A profound change came over Yinn after that escapade. He submerged himself in his studies. He shunned company, preferring solitude. Now and then he would go to the haunted mansion, and gaze at it, lost in thought. It was bandied about that Yinn was bewitched. Nevertheless, he took top honors in the Imperial Examination, just as he said he would. Soon afterwards he was appointed magistrate of Fei and left our town. I failed the examination, went into the family business, and stayed.

Two decades would pass before I crossed paths with Yinn again. Meanwhile, he became a famous judge in the law courts. Though I followed his career with interest we did not correspond. Therefore, a note announcing his return to our town, and inviting me to dinner at our old haunt, both surprised and delighted me.

The tavern we knew in our youth had become a fashionable restaurant, and Yinn had reserved its finest private room. I was astonished by his appearance. Whereas I had grown fat and gray, Yinn seemed hardly a day older than when we last met.

We passed a pleasant evening reminiscing on the old days. Inevitably the conversation turned to the night he spent in the haunted mansion.

"Do you remember that beautiful goblet?" he asked.

"How can I forget?" I chided. "It cost me a feast."

"It has gone back to its rightful owner," Yinn smiled mysteriously, "just as the Fox Faery said it would . . ."

Shortly after he had arrived at Fei, a merchant named Chu invited Yinn to a banquet celebrating the birth of a daughter. At the end of the feast, Chu bade his servant bring out a set of gold goblets for a toast. When the servant appeared with the goblets and one was missing, Chu flew into a rage.

"I've been robbed!" he cried. "These are heirlooms that have been in the family for generations!" And rounding upon his hapless servant, threatened him with a sound flogging unless he produced the missing goblet at once.

Hearing the commotion, Yinn offered to mediate. When he had both sides of the story, he asked to examine one of the goblets.

"I think I may be able to help," he said. He took paper and brush and wrote a note. "Take this to my house and bring what my steward gives you."

The servant flew to the magistrate's house and a short while later returned with a brocaded box.

Yinn presented it to Chu.

To his amazement, the box contained a goblet that exactly matched the others.

"Which brings me to the reason for returning to this town," Yinn added at the end of his recital. "I recently married and plan to buy a certain house and live here." There was a peculiar twinkle in his eyes as he gazed out the window at the mansion looming darkly down the street.

"Surely . . . not . . . that place," I shuddered.

"No other . . ." smiled Yinn. "I've waited a long time . . ."

I couldn't be sure whether he meant he had waited a long time to marry or to buy the house. Yinn pressed a finger to his lips, and then, very deliberately, he winked.

We promised to keep in touch, as people do, but never did. There was talk not long afterward that a stranger had bought the mansion and was actually living in it. However, nothing was done to make it livable, nor was anyone ever seen going in or out. Brave souls who passed it at night claim to have seen lights and heard music and laughter from within. I was curious but never got up the courage to investigate.

During a thunderstorm, one summer's night, the old mansion was struck by lightning and burned to the ground. I never saw Yinn again.

To Be the Best

*L*ao Mu wrestled a bare living from the same few acres of mean earth as his father before him. He was only thirty but seemed older. Too poor to find a wife, he lived alone, with only an old ox for company. Lao Mu grew taciturn, shy, and unsociable. But his love of the earth and his affinity to the wild creatures of the fields, the woods, and the sky sustained him.

Every autumn hunting parties went through the woods that bordered the land he worked, leaving maimed creatures to die in the underbrush in their wake. Lao Mu was cutting down corn stalks one afternoon when a fox streaked out of the woods and disappeared in the direction of his cottage.

"Did you see a fox?" shouted one of the beaters who came pounding after it, ahead of the hunters.

Lao Mu glanced dully at him and went back to what he was doing.

"I say, did you see a fox?" the man roared.

Lao Mu pointed in the opposite direction to where the fox had gone.

"It went that way," shouted the beater, pointing in the direction Lao Mu indicated, as his master joined them.

"Then let's be off before it gets away!" the hunter, who was Lao Mu's landlord, said in a high, affected voice.

Lao Mu watched the hunting party out of the corner of his eye till they were out of sight before sauntering home. A rude fence made of odd bits of wood and sorghum stalks surrounded his cottage. At one side was a lean-to where he kept the ox. Beside it was a haystack, which used to be as neat as a pin. Something had dug a hole in it, causing it to tip forward at a drunken angle. Lao Mu squatted down and peered into the opening partially hidden by whisps of straw. Just as he expected, a large fox was hiding there. Its glossy chestnut colored coat and muzzle, streaked with gray, indicated it was probably quite old. Its right paw was bleeding.

"You'll be safe here, fox," Lao Mu murmured.

The fox lifted its snout and gave its tail a flick as though it understood.

Lao Mu broke up a wuowuoto (a cone-shaped bun made of corn meal) and placed it by the opening in the haystack together with a dish of water. He didn't know what else he could give the poor creature except what he ate himself.

Next morning Lao Mu found a nice fresh cabbage and two oranges on his doorstep. Someone had put them there during the night, for they were wet with dew. He was especially delighted with the oranges, for they did not grow in the north.

In the following days, Lao Mu shared whatever food he had with the injured fox, and mysterious gifts of fruit and vegetables appeared on his doorstep. Sometimes, when he came in at dusk, he found the cottage had been swept. Unseen hands had also lit a fire in the hearth and set a kettle of tea to brew over it. These occurrences did not perturb Lao Mu. He was a simple man who believed one's good or evil deed comes back in an unbroken cycle. He attributed the gifts to the fugitive hiding in his haystack, for he believed foxes could work miracles. He thanked the fox for each gift, and its greenish eyes seemed to respond with pleasure. Thus a friendship began between man and beast.

The fox gradually recovered. One morning when Lao Mu went to the haystack, it was gone. That day Lao Mu went to work with a heavy heart. He had gotten used to the wild creature. He missed talking to it, telling it things he wouldn't dream of revealing to another soul. For under his dull, placid exterior Lao Mu seethed with dreams and aspirations. Though the conversation was one-sided, he sensed the fox understood. Before the fox came into his life, he used to talk to the ox, but the self-absorbed ox had different sensibilities. It was not the same, and Lao Mu felt terribly alone.

Lao Mu spent the day burning corn stalks and returning the ashes to the earth. At dusk he was eager to head home, for he was famished. As he came onto the footpath leading to his cottage, he almost collided with a gentleman dressed in a rich, brown robe topped by a short, gray mantle. The gentleman nodded and smiled.

"Are you lost, sir?" Lao Mu muttered ducking his head.

"Why, no," the other chuckled. "I'm on my way home."

"I've never seen your lordship hereabouts before," stammered Lao Mu.

"I'm not a lordship," the gentleman corrected him with a twinkle. "Call me Mister Huli."

Lao Mu stole a glance at the gentleman whose name sounded like the word for "fox." The man was ageless, with gold flecks dancing in the depths of his greenish eyes that seemed somehow familiar.

"I live nearby," said Mister Huli, taking Lao Mu by the elbow as though they were old friends. "I've been shopping in the village," he said holding out his basket. Lao Mu glanced at its contents in spite of himself. He had forgotten the taste of pork and wine!

"Come, dine with me," invited Mr. Huli. Though every fiber in his body yearned to accept, Lao Mu demured.

"Perhaps your wife is waiting?" asked Mister Huli softly.

Lao Mu shook his head, turning quite red.

"Oh dear!" exclaimed Mister Huli momentarily embarrassed; then he brightened. "In that case there's no reason why you shouldn't come." Mister Huli's grasp on Lao Mu's elbow tightened. A puff of wind blew dust in Lao Mu's face, causing him to blink. Next moment he found himself in a long, narrow room that was simply but elegantly furnished. The wood of table and chairs glowed with warm lights. The scrolls on the walls and the few ornaments scattered about lent the room an air of peace and tranquility. A delicately carved moon door draped with silk curtains separated it from an inner chamber from which wafted the aroma of food being prepared.

"Welcome to my humble home," said Mister Huli. He seated Lao Mu in the place of honor facing south and, placing a tray of sweetmeats and tea before him, urged his guest to take some refreshments while they waited for dinner.

Lao Mu was overwhelmed. The gentry had always treated him with contempt, so he simply did not know how to react. Mister Huli soon put him at his ease. Presently the curtain separating them from the inner room parted, and Mister Huli led the way to a table that groaned with food. The host picked at the food but pressed the choicest morsels upon his guest. The warm honey-colored wine dissolved the last of Lao Mu's reserve.

"Either I'm dreaming," he babbled, "or I'm tipsy!"

Lao Mu woke on his kang (or sleeping platform), not quite sure whether he had dreamed the events he remembered so vividly or whether they had really happened.

It was not till the north wind was blowing that he met Mister Huli again. The old gentleman showed Lao Mu the cache of roots and herbs he had gathered that day, naming each and comfortably describing its medicinal properties.

"I could show you many things. There is wealth in those woods, if one has the knowledge," said Mister Huli, fixing Lao Mu with a meaningful gaze. "And an opportunity to serve one's fellow man too." he concluded, twirling a mysterious looking root between his fingers. All the blood rushed to Lao Mu's head. Everything he knew, he learned by trial and error. There was so much he longed to know but lacked someone to ask. Mr. Huli seemed approachable, but admitting ignorance to oneself is one thing whereas putting it into words for another's ear is something else.

Sensing his hesitation, Mister Huli lowered the hood of his cloak so that only his greenish eyes showed. "We shall talk again," he said with laughter in his voice. A wind came up, and he disappeared into the swirling dust.

Lao Mu was restless in the short, dark winter days that followed. He went into the woods in search of the herbs Mister Huli had shown him, but it was hard-going, for he did not know where to look. Thus, he was overjoyed when he came upon Mister Huli on a similar errand.

"Ah! We are well met indeed," Mister Huli chortled. "You can help me. I need a pair of strong hands to dig some roots," and he held out his scarred right hand to Lao Mu. "It's not much use," he sighed rucfully.

Lao Mu wanted to say something appropriate but couldn't find the words, so he nodded. The two went deep into the woods, Mister Huli pointing out this and that as they went. Lao Mu's mind raced after him, committing every word to memory. As the sun dipped beneath the horizon Mister Huli announced, "You will dine with me. Afterward we will sample a tea made from roots you helped me gather."

Lao Mu bobbed his head in eager consent. He had learned so much that afternoon, he thirsted for more.

Later, over tea, Lao Mu listened, mesmerized, while Mister Huli talked.

Out of the blue Mister Huli asked, "If you could have one wish, what would it be?"

Startled, Lao Mu blurted out the first thing that came to mind.

". . . To be . . . the best . . ."

Once spoken, those words made him squirm.

"What do you mean by the best?" Mister Huli asked softly, but his question seemed like an explosion.

Lao Mu searched the room for an answer. Mr. Huli followed his gaze.

Watching his parents work themselves to death, Lao Mu swore he would not end up the same way. Being the best was having a life like his landlord, Wang, whose house he visited timidly once every quarter to pay his rent and taxes.

Finally he mumbled, "To have . . . land . . . To be . . . respected . . . To live decently . . ."

Mr. Huli's face clouded momentarily, then his voice sounded in Lao Mu's brain, "I will teach you, if you put yourself entirely in my hands. But," he warned, "knowledge is a two-edged sword that can either enrich or destroy you . . ."

"Command me, Master!" cried Lao Mu falling on his knees and banging his head against the ground.

Mister Huli raised him gently.

"No need for groveling," he admonished.

Lao Mu's education began at once. Mister Huli appeared at dusk each day, and the next instant, Lao Mu would find himself in the older man's book-lined study.

Mister Huli opened a whole new world to Lao Mu. He discoursed on the past and the present and how that knowledge could be used to gain an inkling of the future. But Mister Huli was also practical. He taught Lao Mu how to nurture the land, to rotate crops, where to dig for water. Lao Mu soaked up everything like a sponge. When winter faded into spring he was eager to put what he learned into practice. During the season of toil Mr. Huli did not appear. However, a fox came to the edge of the woods from time to time as if to watch him from a distance. Next autumn, Lao Mu's niggardly scrap of land responded with a bountiful harvest.

When the gray pall of acrid smoke from slash burning filled the air, Mister Huli returned.

"Master," Lao Mu cried, running to greet him. "I have such news!"

For the first time in his life he did not worry about paying his rent and taxes. His larder was full. There were even a few strings of coins hidden under a loose brick in a corner of his kang, earned from selling herbal remedies.

Mister Huli seemed pleased, but there was still much to learn he told Lao Mu. The lessons began again.

Several winters later, Wang, the landlord, fell on hard times, and Lao Mu bought the land he worked at a good price, plus another small parcel that had been lying fallow. Lao Mu's life was changing. His success earned him the villagers' grudging respect. Soon they were going to him for advice on this and that. Even the marriage broker started coming round with offers. Lao Mu took everything in stride. Finally, he thought he was on the way to realizing his dream. However, deep inside there was a nagging feeling that something was missing. He broached the question to his mentor at the first opportunity.

"Master, when will I really be the best?"

Mister Huli's eyebrows rose so high they almost disappeared into his cap.

"It's not a question of 'when,'" he replied, "but how you feel here," and he lay a hand gently over Lao Mu's heart.

"How should I feel?" cried Lao Mu. The only model he had was

Wang, his former landlord. Mister Huli pursed his lips in thought. Lao Mu waited with bated breath for him to speak.

"Perhaps you should be introduced to polite society," Mister Huli finally said.

"When?" inquired Lao Mu eagerly.

"This very evening," Mister Huli grinned. "We shall attend a banquet, which I think you will find . . . instructive . . ."

"But I can't," wailed Lao Mu, "I haven't the clothes and . . ."

Before he could finish, a whirlwind deposited him in the foyer of a grand house. In a mirror he caught a reflection of himself and he couldn't believe his eyes. His face was scrubbed, his hair was lacquered, he was dressed in an elegant brown robe, and a full purse made a pleasant bulge in his pocket. Why, he and Mister Huli might have passed for father and son!

"Do not accept a third cup of wine," said Mister Huli in a low voice, "and do not tarry when I bid you to leave." Before he finished speaking their host was bearing down upon them.

"What shall I do?" stammered Lao Mu in a panic, for their host was none other than Wang.

Mister Huli greeted Wang warmly and introduced Lao Mu as his protégé.

"Have I had the pleasure before?" Wang asked searching Lao Mu's face.

Lao Mu glibly passed himself off as a recent arrival from the south. His impersonation of a gentleman traveling for pleasure was flawless. His manners and his witty repartee drew approving smiles all around. Seated between a man of letters and a man of business, Lao Mu realized how little it took to impress those shallow, venal men. He partook of the endless dishes that were placed before him, but he refused the wine.

When a wine from the south was presented, the unctuous

businessman, noticing his abstinence, pressed a cup upon him. Lao Mu could not refuse.

As the wine trickled down his throat the room filled with a golden glow like sunlight filtered through fog on a winter's day. Lao Mu saw himself, a few years older, building a new house. Not a mansion but a far cry from the cottage he lived in nevertheless. Squares of red paper with the double happiness symbol written in gold adorned doors and windows, signifying an imminent wedding. The golden fog cleared, but the happiness lingered.

"This is indeed a wonderful wine!" he heard himself saying.

"Then you must have more," urged his companion.

Mister Huli's warning sounded in Lao Mu's brain. This is only the second cup, he thought, and drank again. Once again a golden mist enveloped him.

This time he saw himself older still, living in the mansion where he was feasting. His wildest dream had come true! Lao Mu saw himself swaggering through the rooms. Everything was his. Flatterers dogged his steps, hanging on his every word. Finally he was the best. Suddenly the scene changed. Fawning smiles turned into looks of cunning, greed, envy, and hate. Grasping hands plucked at him from all sides like ravenous birds of prey.

He was relieved when the vision faded.

"They've all gone to the gaming tables," murmured his table companion. "The two of us must finish this excellent wine . . ."

Before Lao Mu could refuse, the man had refilled his cup. He downed it shakily, in spite of Mister Huli's warning. Instantly, choking gray fog enveloped him, filling him with such dread that he began to weep.

"I didn't think you were the sort that weeps in his cups," his companion chuckled nastily. "Come. A spot of gambling will cheer you!"

At that moment Mister Huli's voice sounded loud and clear.

"Come with me!"

Mister Huli was waiting at the door, stern and unsmiling, but the other was equally insistent.

Lao Mu was drawn to the noise and gaiety of the gaming tables like a moth to a flame.

"Come at once!" Mister Huli sounded angry.

"Just one throw of the dice!" Lao Mu cried defiantly.

The mist before his eyes dispersed. He watched the dice roll across the table as if through the wrong end of a telescope. A deluge of voices overwhelmed him. He watched helplessly as hands snatched up the coins he threw on the table, then seized his purse.

"No!" he shouted, striking out blindly at those nearest him. "You can't take everything I've got!"

An ominous silence fell upon the crowd.

"Thrash him!" his host was the first to break the silence.

The veneer of civility fell away with horrible swiftness. They gave Lao Mu a sound beating before tossing him out of the house.

Bruised, his fine clothes in tatters, Lao Mu trudged home. The lamp was trimmed, the fire lit, and a kettle of tea simmered over the flames when he arrived. Lao Mu never thought he could be so glad to be beside his quiet hearth. It came to him that all he needed was within his own four walls, and the best that life can offer is a tranquil heart.

THE FOXES

Wong Shung's troubles began with the war. The invaders left his town in shambles, but he stayed on. Being a good cabinet maker, he was sure of a reasonable living once reconstruction began. While the town was still reeling, stragglers from the warring armies descended upon it like locusts. What they could not carry away they destroyed. Wong Shung watched helplessly as his home and shop were reduced to ashes. Still Wong Shung would not budge from the place generations of Wongs called home. Misfortune comes in threes. When the plague carried off his family, all he could think of was staying alive. He tied a few possessions he salvaged from the ruins of his home in a bundle, strapped it to his back, and trudged out of the town. Being a frugal man, the cache of coins hidden under the floor of his bed chamber made a comforting bulge in his pocket. A craftsman can make a living anywhere, Wong Shung reassured himself.

The road that led out of the town was crowded with people leaving for the same reason. Wong Shung had no plans except to leave the place that had become too painful to live in. Ten miles out, the road forked. He unstrapped the load from his back and sat down to gnaw a dry bun, and to figure out which way to go.

"Hey, brother!" a stranger shouted. "Come with us! There's a rich town down the road. We'll all make a living there!"

Wong Shung shook his head. Too many people were headed in that direction. He would be better off taking the road that branched off the other way.

The road ribboned through ruined farmland toward a bluish-purple smudge of mountains on the horizon. The farm houses he passed were burned out shells. The light began to fade from the sky. Birds gossiping in the trees fell silent. The wind lowed like a desolate ghost in the black emptiness that engulfed him. Wong Shung sat down in the lee of a huge boulder at the side of the road. He was discovering how ill-prepared he had been when he set out, for he had eaten all the food earlier in the day. In spite of the rumblings of his stomach, he wrapped himself in his cloak and, pillowing his head on his belongings, tried to sleep.

As he drifted off, a noise woke him. For a moment he lay quite still, until his sluggish brain told him what he heard was the hoof beat of approaching horses dragging some kind of vehicle. Wong Shung quickly hefted his possessions, pulled his voluminous cloak over them, and retreated behind an untidy stack of sorghum leaves and stalks in the field nearby. Within minutes a pair of black horses pulling a carriage, traveling without lights, careened around a bend in the road. It came to an abrupt stop near the spot where Wong Shung lay shivering with fright.

The driver leaped off as agile as a cat. First he went over to his horses, whose muzzles he stroked tenderly, whispering to them as though they were children. Then he turned to the fields and stood sniffing the air.

"Come out, come out, whoever you are," he called in an odd sing-song. He seemed to stare right at Wong Shung.

Wong Shung scarcely breathed. He screwed his eyes tight, as though by shutting him out the cloaked figure standing at the edge of the road would disappear.

The man chuckled. "I know you're there . . ."

These days it pays to be cautious, Wong Shung thought. The man might be a heartless brigand who would just as soon rob and kill you as give you the time of day! Wong Shung would have burrowed into the ground if he could. Since he could not, he lay like a limp rag, hoping the other would go away. Behind his tight shut lids, every sound became magnified. The man had stepped back to the coach, talking to someone in a low voice. Just as he thought the coach was about to move on, a foot landed lightly beside his head. Next moment, a hand seized Wong Shung by the hair and hauled him to his feet.

"Well, what have we here?" chortled his captor.

"Just a poor wayfarer, my Lord," quavered Wong Shung. "Please don't hurt me! I can't bear pain!"

"My Lord!" the man mimicked. A woman's tinkling laugh issued from the darkened coach. Wong Shung tried to struggle free, but the other quite easily lifted him off the ground and dragged him on tiptoes toward the coach.

"I won't hurt you," said the coachman in a good-humored voice, "if you promise not to run away."

Wong Shung quickly nodded. The other pinned Wong Shung against the black lacquered side of the coach with his body, blocking any possibility of escape.

"What did you find, brother dear?" the young woman's voice sounded from within the coach.

The man pressed his face close to Wong Shung's. "A man," he replied shortly.

"What is he like?"

"Medium."

"What on earth does that mean?" the young woman's voice rose a pitch.

Wong Shung thought it meant "ordinary," the way people use words such as "nice" and "pretty" when they really mean something could be better. In a flash of anger, he tried to push the man aside, thinking he could bolt into the night. But the man was too strong for him. One long-fingered hand coiled around his neck and the other seized him by the seat of his pants. Next moment, Wong Shung landed on the seat beside the driver's with such a thud that he felt his brain had been jarred loose. In a daze, he realized the coach was careering down the road. The driver whipped his team into a fine froth. Wong Shung hung on to his perch till his knuckles ached. It was all he could do to keep from being flung off. The driver shrieked a peculiar sounding song at the sky, which roused flocks of sleeping birds into noisy flight.

Finally the driver allowed the horses to slacken their pace. Wong Shung breathed a sigh of relief.

"Who are you, sir?" Wong Shung gasped. Now that his eyes had adjusted to the dark, Wong Shung saw a narrow face with high cheekbones; a long, delicate nose; and a wide mouth.

"You may call me Fox, for Fox Faery," said the man. Jutting his chin at the coach he added, "She is my sister, Hu Mei."

"You make sport of me, sir," Wong Shung did his best to sound indignant. Ancient foxes who take human form at night only exist in fairy tales, he told himself. Nevertheless, he shot his companion another nervous glance. Except for the eyes that seemed to pierce Wong Shung's very soul, his captor was no different from any other human.

"Where are you taking me?"

The driver studied him before answering, "Anywhere is better than where you came from."

Wong Shung was at a loss for a rebuttal.

"Don't sulk," said the driver over his shoulder. "There is nothing as unappetizing as a balky guest who is expected to stay a while."

Wong Shung's hair stood on end.

"It's no good holding me for ransom," he said breathlessly. "There isn't a soul left in the family to pay. You might as well let me go." The driver shook his head and sighed.

"Wong Shung, you are such a ninny! Relax!"

Wong Shung's eyes went wide. How did the man know his name! The man chuckled. "I know a lot about you."

Fox shook the reigns, and the coach went barreling through the night again. Wong Shung was glad when it came to a halt in front of a large house. Fox leaped off and hurried inside. Presently he returned with a lighted lamp. He reached up and plucked Wong Shung off the coach.

"Light the way for my sister," he said, handing him the lamp. "I'll see to the horses. The servants are asleep."

He held the coach door open, and a heavily cloaked young woman alighted.

For a moment her hood cast a deep shadow across her face. As she paused and turned, the light caught a small, heart-shaped face, dominated by a pair of luminous, amber-colored eyes; a small mouth; and a pert but stubborn little nose. She was a classic beauty. Fox's booted foot, applied firmly to Wong Shung's rump, propelled him into the house ahead of the young woman.

The young woman directed him down a long corridor to a room. The air was stale. The furniture was shrouded in sheets heavy with dust. The young woman surveyed the huge, unlived-in room disdainfully. With an imperious gesture she indicated she wanted a window opened. Wong Shung leaped to comply, conscious of being observed as he wrestled with the rusty latch. The window swung open suddenly. Wong Shung turned almost colliding with the young woman who was right behind him. Holding the lamp high, she examined him as if he were an exotic animal.

Just then Fox entered from somewhere in the depths of the house.

"What took so long, dear brother?" the young woman asked petulantly without taking her eyes off Wong Shung. The fingers of one slender hand drumming the top of a table beside her showed her impatience.

"The horses had to be seen to," replied Fox. "I expect you want to retire . . ." he added.

Hu Mei shrugged impatiently.

Fox took the lamp from her.

"You will sleep in here," he said to Wong Shung, raising the lamp above his head, spinning on his heels to show off the room. "Use the kang or the chaise, whichever you prefer. Do not touch anything else. And don't even think of escape . . ."

He escorted his sister from the room, leaving Wong Shung in the dark.

Now that he had a good look at his strange captors, Wong Shung was less afraid. They certainly fit tales about Fox Faeries who take the form of a beautiful woman or a dashing young man. However, he resolutely dismissed the notion as nonsense. It was easier to believe the pair were merely using superstition to throw him off balance. Meanwhile, having a roof over his head was far better than sleeping in the open. As Wong Shung went to shut the window against the night air, he noticed shadows moving against a lighted pane across the courtyard. Voices carried in the stillness.

"Are you sure this one is suitable?" Wong Shung heard Hu Mei say in a lilting voice. He could hear her brother's voice indistinctly from somewhere further in the room.

Whatever he said evidently displeased his sister. Her tone became quite angry, even shrill. The shadows flickering across the patch of light showed that both were agitated. As he came closer, Wong Shung heard Fox say in a placating tone, ". . . but he has other qualities. You need someone who . . ." They moved out of earshot again. Then the light went out.

Stretched out on the kang, Wong Shung pondered what he had overheard. He was certain brother and sister had been discussing him. The man who called himself Fox obviously fancied he knew a great deal about him, but it was Hu Mei's opinion that mattered, and it had to do with his appearance. Instinctively his hand went to his face.

"What is the matter with the way I look?" Wong Shung wondered. A fortune-teller once said his high forehead and bushy eyebrows that met across the bridge of his nose were signs of talent and intelligence. And he was an excellent craftsman and wood carver, even if he said so himself. It's true his head is squarish, but his heavy jaw indicates strong-mindedness. (So far, so good.) But the squat nose with the flared nostrils, the thick, dark lips, especially the round eyes undid all that. They made him look bovine. The last image in his mind as he drifted off was Hu Mei scrutinizing him, head tilted mockingly to one side.

The sun was high when Wong Shung awoke. A three-tiered food carrier stood on a table with utensils laid out for one. A jug of water and a basin stood just inside the door. For the moment he was too famished to consider anything but food. He wolfed a plate of warm meat dumplings and a bowl of noodles in a rich broth, followed by two bowls of an excellent tea, before he read the note on the table.

"My sister and I hope you will be comfortable in these surroundings. As soon as we decide on a commission, we shall communicate it to you personally. In the meantime, our servants will see to your needs."

A quick look around the room revealed that under the dust covers, the once elegant furniture was dilapidated from long neglect. It was evident that new furniture was needed. However, one does not kidnap a craftsman to furnish one's house, thought Wong Shung indignantly. The more he thought about it, the angrier he got. The door to the room was lightly shut. He opened it and yelled for the servants loudly, but no one came. Undistinguishable sounds sent him darting down the hallway, shouting, opening and shutting doors. The rooms on either side were all dusty and empty. Finally it dawned upon him he was alone.

Who are these people? What do they want? Why do they live in isolation? One question led to another. What if they are Fox Faeries? Fear reared its ugly head again. Wong Shung decided he must make the best of the daylight hours, when Fox Faeries are helpless, to get as far away from this place as he could. He retraced his footsteps to the room where he had slept, picked up his bundle, and went down the corridor in the opposite direction, looking for the entrance foyer he remembered from the night before. In one room Wong Shung came upon a red wood cabinet with shiny brass fittings that looked new but had a broken latch. Curiosity made him look inside. What he saw made Wong Shung's jaw drop. He leaned his head against the cupboard, took a few deep breaths, and looked again. Inside were gold ingots stacked in a pyramid. There was more gold than he dared dream of, and it was within reach!

"Gold is the key to the future!" flashed through Wong Shung's mind. Suddenly, everything was possible.

Wong Shung tiptoed across the room with his heart in his mouth, and pressed his ear to the window. All he heard was sparrows chirping and wind rustling the trees. He tried a door that led outside and opened it a crack. The narrow strip of courtyard that came into view was as neglected as the rest of the house. There was no sign of another living soul. Still, he had to be sure. He stole across the courtyard to a large window with an elaborately carved frame that must have been the room where Fox and his sister had been the night before. Silence. He wet a fingertip with spittle and applied it to the rice paper window covering, working it gently until he made a hole large enough to peep through. Two large foxes lay curled on the floor, sound asleep.

Wong Shung broke into a sweat. He hurried back to the cupboard, dumped his precious tools on the floor, rolled up as many gold ingots as he could carry in some clothes, and strapped the bundle on his back. Instead of trying to find the entrance to the house, he clambered up an old chestnut tree in the middle of the courtyard, then swung onto the roof. He slithered lizard-fashion onto its peak and looked over the edge. A clump of trees screened the house from open fields beyond. Wong Shung slid down the other side and dropped lightly onto the ground. He had no idea where he was, nor did he care. His only thought was to get as far away as possible from the foxes' house before sunset.

Wong Shung tried to comfort himself with the thought that it was war and its awful aftermath that forced him to steal. Besides, what good is gold to a pair of foxes?

But was he sure Fox and Hu Mei were the sleeping foxes he saw and not rich eccentrics? An inner voice reminded Wong Shung there is one set of laws for the poor and another for the rich. The rich would exact a terrible penalty if he were caught.

Pursued by disquieting thoughts, Wong Shung discovered that a thief is friendless. Afraid of being caught, constantly on guard against those who might try to separate him from his ill-gotten gains, he avoided the main thoroughfares. In spite of the gold, he was cold, and hungry, subsisting on wild berries, sleeping in abandoned fields.

Finally, Wong Shung struck a bargain with a good-natured muleteer. In exchange for loading and unloading his cart along the way, the muleteer agreed to take Wong Shung as far as he was going. Weeks later, Wong Shung arrived at a depot along the Grand Canal.

He exchanged one gold ingot for cash at a merchant house and bought passage on a barge leaving for the south.

The northern plain where he was born was far behind, but Wong Shung was still fearful. He wandered restlessly until he found a quiet little town near Lake Dong Ting and settled. With a small part of his gold, he bought new tools and set up a workshop. The rest he buried under the floor of his house. He worked hard, lived frugally, and did not seek the company of other people.

Wong Shung gradually became renowned not only as a cabinet maker but as a wood carver. Hu Mei's image had been so indelibly imprinted upon his mind that he was compelled to reproduce it in wood carvings of such refinement, beauty, and grace that the pieces seemed to breathe. Before long, his work was in such demand that he had to take apprentices to help fulfill his commissions.

Wong Shung's art became his life. The rewards it brought were only a secondary consideration. He was known as a pleasant man, with a ready smile and a kindly word for everyone. However, a peculiar stillness set him apart. He was hard to know. Wong Shung became a recluse.

Ten years passed.

Late one night there was a knock on the door. Wong Shung never received visitors after dark. However, a new apprentice answered the door. A moment later he announced a gentleman to see the master. Wong Shung was about to rebuke the boy, but the visitor had already followed him into the room. Wong Shung stood with his mouth open as the man who called himself Fox crossed the space between them in a few quick strides.

"I am delighted to see you," cried Fox as he pressed a coin into the apprentice's hand and waved him from the room. He waited till they were alone before he picked up a candle to examine Wong Shung's face.

"You've changed," murmured Fox.

Wong Shung's face was lined. The glossy black hair was mostly gray. Furthermore, his eyes were weak, and the tremor in his hands forced him to work less than he liked. On the other hand, Fox looked not a day older than Wong Shung remembered.

"I'm a Fox Faery," Fox twinkled mischievously, reading Wong Shung's thoughts. "We neither age nor die. However," he added, beaming, "you are exactly the way I hoped to find you! Successful. Respected. Well-to-do."

Wong Shung did not know what to make of that remark. He screwed up his courage and took the plunge.

"I'm sorry I stole your gold," he blurted. "I was desperate. I will pay you back with interest if you will allow me a day or two to make arrangements . . ."

His visitor let out a short, derisive laugh.

"If I wanted the gold, I would take it," he said hopping nimbly from one spot to the other, landing unfailingly on each of Wong Shung's hiding places under the floor.

Wong Shung blanched. Through a great buzzing in his ears, he heard Fox say the gold was payment in advance.

"What do you want?" quavered Wong Shung.

Fox smiled broadly, in no hurry to divulge what was on his mind.

"In exchange for the gold, which is of no use to us," he began teasingly, "my sister and I crave that which is of no use to you."

While Wong Shung pondered that riddle, Fox padded about the room, examining various likenesses of his sister, both finished and in progress. He stopped before a life-size sculpture of the young woman dancing, turning it this way and that to catch the light. It was the first of countless representations of Hu Mei that Wong Shung had made. In his own mind it was his finest. For that reason he guarded it jealously.

"My sister will be flattered," murmured Fox appreciatively.

Wong Shung was dismayed. If his visitor demanded it, he would have to give it up, and its loss would break his heart.

The conversation took another tack.

"It is time my sister was wed . . ." announced Fox, his gaze traveling from the statue to Wong Shung.

Wong Shung was single. All these years he had pined for an ideal mate, without ever identifying what it was he yearned for. In a flash, he knew. That Fox would bring up the matter at all was a sign that whatever differences might exist were no longer important.

For a brief moment Wong Shung was about to ask for Hu Mei's hand. Then he glimpsed himself reflected in the glass door of a cupboard, and reddened. He was old before his time. He wished he were young and vigorous again, but it was too late. Fox watched him, a knowing smile tugging at his lips.

Wong Shung brusquely thrust that impossible thought from his mind.

"You will need the gold for your sister's dowry," Wong Shung said in an effort to divert Fox's attention from the statue.

Fox settled himself in a chair with a weary sigh.

"It's not as simple as that," he began. "You see me as I was during the period known in your history as the Warring States . . ."

"That was more than a thousand years ago," breathed Wong Shung, "nobody lives that long."

"Fox Faeries do," said Fox. "My sister is a little younger. However, being forever young and beautiful becomes a burden eventually."

"A burden I would give my soul for," muttered Wong Shung.

Fox continued as though he hadn't heard.

"By day we are foxes. At night we are like you, except we are doomed to be mimics and observers. My sister and I have wandered every inch of All Under Heaven, tasted all the pleasures, but we are unfulfilled. We long to be real participants of the human condition."

Wong Shung thought to himself, if I could have youth and an infinite lifespan, I would ask for nothing more. Fox picked that thought right out of Wong Shung's mind.

"Fear usually separates my kind from yours. Evidently, you are an exception . . ."

Wong Shung was not listening. His thoughts were racing.

"Love will overcome everything," he murmured.

"I believe you are truly devoted to my sister." Fox shook Wong Shung gently by the shoulders. "Eternal youth is yours if you marry my sister."

Fox's last remark sounded like a clarion. Wong Shung did not hesitate to accept.

"You will go with me this very night to where my sister is waiting. There you will be wed. You will live with her and care for her. I shall be away," his gesture indicated his travels were unimportant except to himself. "My sister will help you become a creature of the night like us . . ."

"What will happen then?" stammered Wong Shung.

"Why, you will have the immortality you crave. Let us seal the pact." Fox's smile felt like a cold hand clutching his heart.

Fox pulled out a hairpin from his top knot, stabbed his thumb and bade Wong Shung do the same. They pressed their bloody thumbs together, and the deed was done.

Wong Shung's eyes grew heavy. He shut them for an instant. When he opened them he was in a different place. Everything was new and exciting. Instead of his dusty smock he wore a bridegroom's ceremonial robe. He snatched up a mirror and gaped at the reflection. He was as he had been when he was twenty, only his features were softened, more refined.

"Come," Fox chuckled from across the room. "You mustn't keep your bride waiting!"

Wong Shung and Hu Mei were married. Fox departed as soon as was polite after the ceremony.

"You have what you desire," he said, holding his sister's hand in both his, "now I must seek mine."

"Go in peace," she smiled serenely.

Though an uncommon passion bound them, for a while Wong Shung could not adapt to the Fox Faery's life entirely. During the day, when Hu Mei sank into a deathlike sleep, the newly acquired ability to be somewhere merely by wishing it allowed Wong Shung to visit the house where he had lived and worked. Unrecognizable, he mingled with art fanciers who thronged his studio offering ridiculous prices for works he had left behind. Wong Shung's sudden disappearance was quickly construed as death. Death made him legend, which itself is a kind of immortality.

Wong Shung and Hu Mei lived in the passionate contentment of lovers for whom time had no meaning. As Wong Shung adapted to his new life, like a butterfly emerging from a cocoon, Hu Mei began to age. Imperceptible at first, the process accelerated once it took hold. Hu Mei was serene. However, Wong Shung was filled with anguish as his beautiful young wife withered before his eyes.

"You made a bargain," Hu Mei reminded Wong Shung gently. "You agreed to take on the burden of endless life that I might find love and everlasting peace . . ."

Hu Mei disappeared into the ether, but Wong Shung lives on . . . and on . . . and on . . .

THE PEAR TREE

*F*armer Chang went into town once a year, and he went in style. For days before, his orchard and farmhouse buzzed with activity. The farmer's shiny pate glowed importantly as he stamped from house to yard to fields and back again, shouting orders left and right, sending his farmhands scurrying in all directions.

"Everything must be just so, or there'll be the devil to pay!" he shouted.

The mule cart was spruced up with a coat of fresh red lacquer. The mule was scrubbed and curried till its coat glistened. Its harness was polished and hung with copper bells that jingled merrily, and festooned with ribbons that matched the color of the cart. The groom, a boy of twelve, was told to get a haircut and a bath and given a new cotton jacket befitting the servant of a prosperous farmer.

On a crisp autumn day, after his pears were harvested, Farmer Chang loaded his cart and set out for town. As he passed through the streets, harness bells jingle-jangling, the beetle-browed farmer perched high on his cart cracked his whip, while the groom piped in a high, reedy voice, "Buy Farmer Chang's pears! Farmer Chang's pears! Best in the county!"

"Best in the world is more like it," muttered Farmer Chang, and ordered the boy to shout louder.

"Put some feeling into it! And shake that bell harder! People must know Farmer Chang has come to town!"

People stopped on the sidewalks or poked their heads out of windows to watch the bright red cart pass.

"Oooh, look how fat and prosperous Farmer Chang has become," someone observed.

"What a fine mule and cart," exclaimed another.

A few waved and shouted greetings, but Farmer Chang looked neither right nor left. His eyes were stony in his expressionless face. He wanted no truck with the townsfolk, for they had not been so welcoming when he was down on his luck. Now he only wanted their money.

Farmer Chang had worked hard for as long as he could remember. He started with a tiny plot of land and a few miserable trees from which he barely made a living, but he dreamed of developing the finest pears in the county. Day and night he thought of nothing but his trees. His wife, a quiet, patient soul, toiled with him, nurturing the trees as if they were children. The years blurred into one another. Poverty and toil took their toll. One autumn just as the pears were turning luscious and golden, Farmer Chang's wife took ill and did not stir from her bed. Her husband ranted at her furiously. She gazed at him with eyes filled with such indefinable sadness that he finally sputtered into silence.

"Perhaps I will be more help to you from beyond," she whispered. Turning her face to the wall, breath left her.

She was buried without ceremony at the foot of the orchard, whence, according to the necromancer, she would continue to oversee Farmer Chang's little domain. He marked her resting place with a small mound, for ground is precious, and placed before it a blank stone tablet.

"What's the point of engraving it?" he reasoned. "I know she's there and so does she. It's enough."

The woman's death did not touch Farmer Chang. Instead he was vexed that she died just when he needed an extra pair of hands, for the crop was heavy that year.

That was the turning point in Farmer Chang's career. From then on each crop was better than the one before. As the fame of his pears spread, Farmer Chang grew prosperous. He bought more land, planted more trees, built himself a proper house, and hired farmhands. Though he was successful, his soul shriveled. He cared for no one. He had no friends. His orchard was his life, and the money he earned he hoarded in a secret place under the floor tiles of his room.

Farmer Chang's mule cart meandered through the town till it reached the market square. There it stopped. The Farmer and the groom raised an awning over the cart to shade the pears from the midday sun.

"I'm ready for business!" the Farmer announced in a loud voice, holding up a pear in each hand for all to see. Many of the townsfolk had followed the Farmer as he made his stately progress through the streets. Business was brisk, though buyers were aghast at the price.

"You want my pears, you pay my price," sneered Farmer Chang as he snatched the coins from his customers, dispensing his wares as though they were blessings.

A mendicant Monk came to the square begging food. He looked at the farmer's fruit longingly.

"The man's prosperous," thought the Monk. "Surely he wouldn't miss one pear . . ."

He joined the queue. When he finally stood before Farmer Chang, he bowed, saying in a low voice, "Master, I'm hungry and thirsty . . . In the name of Buddha would you spare me a pear?"

Farmer Chang's eyes snapped wide with amazement. Was he hearing things?

Clearly not. For there was the Monk, repeating what he had just said in a thin, whiny voice.

"What! . . . What! . . ." gasped Farmer Chang. "Give away a pear!"

He had never heard anything so preposterous!

The Monk went on bowing and begging. His ragged robe sent up such a stench that people began to back away. Seeing that he might lose customers because of this wretched fellow, Farmer Chang bellowed, "Go away, you cabbage-faced bundle of misery! Get away from here!"

The Monk just went on bowing and muttering.

"Take care how you provoke me," cried Farmer Chang, "or I'll thrash you within an inch of your life!"

Farmer Chang meant what he said, but the Monk was equally stubborn. Even when the Farmer's whip came whistling down on his head and shoulders, he stood his ground. The lash drew blood. There was a cry of outrage from the crowd, but nobody tried to interfere.

A gentleman passing by in a litter heard the commotion, called out to his bearers to stop, and alighted to see what was afoot. He was disgusted by what he saw.

"Stop!" he shouted.

Farmer Chang's whip faltered in midair.

"What's the meaning of this violence?" demanded the gentleman.

A dozen voices piped up immediately. The Gentleman pieced together the story as best he could.

"If that's all the fuss is about," he said, eyeing Farmer Chang contemptuously, "I'll buy him a pear."

He selected a large pear and threw a coin to Farmer Chang. Then, gently leading the Monk away from the cart, handed him the fruit.

"Remember me in your prayers," the Gentleman said as he climbed back into his litter and went his way.

The Monk took his pear to the opposite side of the square. Sitting on the ground, he wolfed it, stem, core, and all, except for one tiny seed. He found a stick and used it to dig a small hole in the hard packed earth, laid the seed in it, and covered it with loose soil. From a shop nearby he begged a cup of water and poured it over the newly planted seed.

"What are you doing, Master?" asked the shopkeeper.

"This town has been good to me," replied the Monk. "A kind gentleman gave me a pear when I was hungry and thirsty. I planted its seed so that the fruit might refresh other wayfarers."

"That's a noble thought," the shopkeeper scratched his head, "but the ground is hard and barren; nothing will grow in it."

"It will grow," smiled the Monk.

He sat down beside the spot where the pear seed was planted, shut his eyes, and began to chant.

The Shopkeeper looked on skeptically. Suddenly he thought he saw movement in the earth, as if something was pushing its way up. He rubbed his eyes and looked more closely. A small, white shoot was poking through the soil. The shoot began to grow before his eyes. In a moment it had grown into a sapling with leaves and branches.

"A miracle! A miracle!" the Shopkeeper shouted, beside himself with excitement.

His cries brought people sprinting across the square from every direction to cluster around the Monk. Those who were tardy jostled and tried to climb onto the shoulders of the people in front to catch a glimpse of the magic tree. The Monk went on chanting, oblivious of the hubbub around him. The tree grew. Buds appeared and burst into bloom. The blossoms fell and fruit began to form. Soon the tree was so laden that the boughs were breaking.

Meanwhile, the altercation with the Monk had so upset Farmer Chang that his heart beat painfully and his breath came in short, rapid gasps. He sat down in the shade of his cart, barely able to swallow the cup of tea his frightened groom pressed to his ashen lips.

"Look after the customers," he gasped. "I'll rest a while."

He dozed. He came to with a start, for he no longer heard the boy ringing his bell and shouting his wares. Worst of all, there weren't any customers. He got to his feet shakily and called the boy's name. There was no answer. Then he noticed the crowd at the other side of the square.

"Something terrible has happened," he thought. "I'd best stay with my cart."

However, his curiosity was piqued. He stopped the first person who passed his way and asked what was going on.

"A strange monk planted a magical pear tree that grew and bore fruit right before our eyes," exclaimed the stranger. "Even now he's distributing the fruit. I swear it was the best pear I've ever had!"

"That's impossible," scoffed Farmer Chang. "I grow the best pears . . . in the county . . ." He would have liked to say "the world," but something made him hold back.

"They're better, and they're free," the stranger gloated.

That remark was enough to send Farmer Chang waddling across the square as fast as his legs would carry him. Sure enough, a pear tree stood where there used to be empty space. All around him happy people were munching pears, dribbling juice down their chins and onto their tunics. The same dirty, ragged monk was handing out the fruit.

Farmer Chang hung back for a moment. By then the tree was almost stripped. His curiosity was too much to bear. Farmer Chang sidled up to the Monk with an outstretched hand and a sheepish grin.

"Ah! Now I can return your kindness, sir," bowed the Monk.

He plucked the last pear and handed it to the Farmer.

Farmer Chang tucked the fruit in his sleeve and beat a fast retreat. He was dying to taste it, but no one must see him. For, didn't he grow the best in the county, if not the world? He ducked behind his cart, out of sight of the crowd, and bit into his pear. It was as crisp, sweet, and juicy as his own. In fact, he couldn't tell the difference. He gobbled it down in a fever of excitement until only the seeds were left. He took them into the light and examined them carefully. They were identical to those he developed through years of trial and error. A dreadful thought entered his mind.

"It's a trick," he muttered under his breath.

Then he noticed his mule was loose, for one of the tracers of his cart had been broken off.

With a wildly beating heart, he raised himself on tiptoes, and peered into his cart.

"It's empty!" he cried. A blinding light flashed before his eyes. The Monk had somehow stolen his pears. He shouted for his groom, but the boy was gone.

Farmer Chang trotted angrily back across the square. The crowd had dispersed. The Shopkeeper was sweeping up some branches and leaves. Farmer Chang's eyes went round with amazement.

"Where's the Monk?" he stuttered, ". . . and my groom?"

"He left," answered the Shopkeeper. "The boy who helped him distribute the pears went with him."

Some said the Monk went in one direction, others averred he had gone in another. Actually nobody knew. All that was left was a pear tree standing in the corner of the market square, its branches lifted in prayer toward the sky. If one looked closely, one would find flecks of red lacquer embedded so deep in its bark that neither wind nor rain would ever fade it.

WHISKERS
AND
BRIGHT EYES

*S*he called him "Whiskers" because he had the most dashing pair of mustaches she had ever seen. He called her "Bright Eyes" because the laughter in her eyes filled him with joy. They lived in the back of a general store, where the air was always laden with the smell of honey, spices, fruits, and a dozen grains. It was a noisy, dusty, busy place with something going on all the time. But it was warm and dry.

"And food is plentiful," Whiskers pointed out. "It's not easy for a couple of mice to find a place to live in the city."

Bright Eyes agreed everything he said was perfectly true. However, she was a country mouse, who was used to different surroundings. She missed the changing colors and smells of the seasons. Here it was always the same. In the country she came and went as she pleased. Here she had to be careful. Particularly of the giant whom Whiskers grandly referred to as his "Pet." He was huge. Why, his toe was longer than her body! He was so tall that Bright Eyes had never seen his face, for a gigantic paunch that jiggled and swayed whenever he moved hid his face from view. But Whiskers claimed he glimpsed it once.

"For a human, it's not a bad face," said Whiskers stroking his mustaches.

"Does the Pet have mustaches?" blinked Bright Eyes.

Whiskers glanced at her archly. "Pets don't as a rule."

They always knew when the Pet was coming because the ground shook, their furniture rattled, and their wedding picture on the wall promptly went askew.

"Oh dear! Oh dear!" cried Bright Eyes. "There it goes again."

She righted the portrait with a sigh. "Oh how I long for the peace of open spaces."

For that day, the Pet was stomping about and shouting more than usual. In fact, the place was more a-bustle than she had ever seen.

"It's alright," soothed Whiskers. "The Pet is happy."

"Happy!" exclaimed Bright Eyes, covering her ears. "Oooh, what ghastly noises he makes!"

"That's called 'singing,'" Whiskers wrinkled his nose. "Personally, I don't much care for it, but humans do it when they're happy. Aren't you glad I'm a mouse?"

He drew Bright Eyes to the entrance of their burrow, and together they peered out at the goings-on. Some of the clerks were sweeping and scrubbing. Others were hanging up red bunting. Still others were pasting squares of red paper with gold squiggles onto the walls. The Pet darted here and there with remarkable swiftness for such a large person, overseeing everything in a great booming voice, bursting into snatches of song from time to time, in a high, shrill voice.

"See those red squares they're putting on the walls?" Whiskers pointed out for Bright Eyes. "That's the symbol for double happiness. It means the Pet is getting married." He put his arm around his little wife and gave her shoulders a squeeze. "We are going to have a Pettess."

"A Pettess!" giggled Bright Eyes. "Maybe things will be different from now on."

And things were different. It grew quieter. There was less dust in the air. The Pet seemed less heavy footed and didn't shout quite as much as he used to. However, he made it up with his singing, which put the two mice's teeth on edge. The Pettess glided about in dainty slippers embroidered with bright red peonies and glossy green leaves. Bright Eyes particularly liked the scent of rose water that followed wherever she went. The Pettess spoke with a soft musical voice. She was always unhurried and calm. She had the alcove opposite the mice's burrow cleaned and painted and made into a shrine for the Kitchen God. Every morning she placed little dishes of fruit and cakes on the altar, lit candles and incense, and prayed for the safety and happiness of all those who lived under their roof. At night when the store was shuttered, the two mice would venture forth to nibble on the food left for the god.

Bright Eyes was dubious about touching the offerings at first, but it was hard to resist Whiskers' reasoning.

"The Pettess will think the Kitchen God ate it," he said, "and she'll be pleased. Humans are not very smart. We know an image drawn on a piece of paper can't eat."

As time went by the two mice got bolder, and then they got careless. One day the Pettess placed a dish of fresh millet cakes on the Kitchen God's altar. They smelled so good that Bright Eyes was on pins and needles waiting for the day to end.

"You mustn't go out until it's dark," cautioned Whiskers, for he could see mischief gleaming in the other's eyes, as he prepared to go out foraging.

Bright Eyes gave her head a toss, and retorted, "You're going out."

"I'm the man of the house," replied Whiskers, deliberately weighting the word "man," "It's my job to bring home the bacon—or whatever."

"Then bring some millet cake," Bright Eyes' chin went up at a challenging angle.

"I will," promised Whiskers as he peered out the burrow to see if the coast was clear. "But you must wait till after dark."

"By then they'll be stale," Bright Eyes stamped her foot. "Or maybe the Kitchen God will have eaten them!"

"Don't be silly!" scoffed Whiskers. He gave Bright Eyes a quick peck on the cheek and scurried out before she could say anything more.

Left alone, Bright Eyes tried to concentrate on her chores, but the scent of those millet cakes drove her to distraction. Stealthy footsteps sprinting past the burrow made her peer out, just in time to see one of the boys who did the sweeping up snatch one of the millet cakes off the altar and stuff it whole into his mouth.

Bright Eyes gasped in horror. At this rate there won't be any left by nightfall!

There wasn't a moment to lose. She streaked out of the burrow, scampered up the altar, and just as she was about to sink her teeth into a millet cake, the Pettess appeared.

"A mouse! A mouse! Aaaaah!" shrieked the Pettess.

The store was turned into bedlam. It was all Bright Eyes could do to dart back into the burrow. She rolled herself into a tiny ball and cowered in a dark corner, as the Pet and his staff went about with brooms and sticks hunting for the mouse. Once Bright Eyes had caught her breath, the dreadful thought came to her that Whiskers was out there. He could be in terrible danger, and it was all her fault. Oh, those hateful millet cakes, she thought. I shall never think of them again if only Whiskers is safe! As a matter of fact, he was. Being wise to human ways, he sauntered home when the commotion died down, as though nothing had happened, with the food he had found, together with a piece of millet cake.

A few days later the Pet brought home a gift that delighted the Pettess no end. She cooed and gurgled and made silly noises at it.

The two mice overheard her say quite distinctly, "Mimi will keep the mice away!"

"They've got a cat!" cried Whiskers and Bright Eyes in unison.

Mimi was small-boned, sleek, and gleaming black, with four white paws and a bib. Two great eyes with yellow crescents in them dominated her small, crafty face. A white spot like a birthmark over the right corner of her mouth gave her a rakish air. She moved with a fluid, regal grace, her eyes like beacons searching out every nook and cranny of the store. It did not take her long to discover where her favorite foods were stored, and the coziest corner to sleep in. Of course, she also discovered where Whiskers and Bright Eyes lived, and made the expected cat noises that pleased the Pet and the Pettess. But Mimi had a mind of her own. She was careful to keep up appearances, making a great show of taking charge of the mouse situation. So long as the mice kept out of her way, she was content to live and let live. With salted fish and pressed duck to tickle her palate, mice were not even an option on her menu.

Nevertheless, Mimi was a worry. Whiskers was particularly concerned about Bright Eyes, who tended to be flighty and careless. The adventure with the millet cakes could have ended in disaster. Though he scolded and she was contrite, Whiskers knew that when the mood for mischief came upon her there was no stopping Bright Eyes. He decided they had to move.

"But where?" cried Bright Eyes.

"I don't know," replied Whiskers stroking his mustaches thoughtfully. "Perhaps somewhere with a view . . ."

That last remark was not lost on Bright Eyes.

"Can we go and live in the country?" chirped Bright Eyes, all agog.

"I said 'a view,'" Whiskers tried to sound noncommittal, "nothing about the country. It's mainly to keep you out of harm's way." He pulled a long face.

Bright Eyes sighed, completely deflated. She knew how much Whiskers liked their present home and how he hated to leave it. If only the Pet hadn't brought Mimi into the house!

Finally Whiskers found an empty burrow in the far corner of the back garden that was almost perfect. To be sure, it was a bit far to carry home the groceries, but there were advantages. There was plenty of sunlight and fresh air. Flowers from spring to autumn would please Bright Eyes. Best of all, Mimi would be far away because the Pettess never let her out of the house.

As summer ripened into autumn Whiskers and Bright Eyes moved into their new abode. That same day a large snake, its scales shimering with gold flecks, slithered into the garden, dusty and tired after a long journey. Finding a cool spot in a bamboo grove, it coiled itself up for a nap. Its presence was noticed at once by the rooster who patroled the garden with a majestic gait. He warned his hens, who noisily rounded up their chicks at once. Their clucking startled the frogs sunning themselves by the pond, who leaped onto the lily pads floating in the center, or vanished into the water. The owl perched in the dark branches of a gnarled old pine snapped awake from a deep sleep. "Who?" he said querulously, swivelling his head this way and that, trying to look alert, except he didn't see well in the light. Whiskers and Bright Eyes, however, were too excited about their new home to notice.

The snake was heavy with food, for she had dined well on two frogs and a bird's egg on the way. She was faintly annoyed by the flurry that her presence caused. All she wanted was sleep. "It's the price one pays for being beautiful," she sighed, for she was vain. "Think green," she told herself, and instantly she was the same color as the bamboo leaves that shaded her. With another sigh, she composed herself for sleep, when something made her open one pale eye just a slit. Then wider and wider.

Two mice were coming out of a burrow.

"How convenient," thought the snake as her eye shut again. She could feel the touch of autumn in the air. It was time to find a winter place. "How delicious!" she murmured as she drifted off. Though she was partial to frogs and eggs, a steady diet of them got tedious. Mouse would be such a nice change! And a place to live afterward. She felt blessed indeed.

One morning after Whiskers had gone out to forage, and Bright Eyes was busily sorting and putting away their provisions for the winter, she was startled by a rustling sound. Someone was coming through the door. Presently a creature stood before her unlike any other she had ever seen.

"Who are you?" shrilled Bright Eyes. "What are you doing in my house?"

"Oh, I am sorry," murmured the snake. Her large, pale eyes quickly took in the room. The hideous furniture and the tasteless pictures will have to go, she thought. But all in good time . . . all in good time. Instead she smiled, showing a pair of glittering fangs. "I thought the house was empty," continued the snake. "I was looking for a place to stay."

"Well, it isn't," replied Bright Eyes a little more sharply than she intended. "Whiskers and I just moved in," she added tartly.

The snake slithered in a little further, her sleek body swaying ever so gently while her inquisitive tongue darted this way and that. "Hhmmm," she hummed softly. "Such a cozy spot you have . . ."

The stranger was making Bright Eyes nervous. The way that slender tongue glided down her face and body made her tremble. But those pale, pale eyes seemed to nail her to the floor so that she could hardly move.

"I'm called Bright Eyes," she stammered. "I'm a mouse."

"I am Fangs," cooed the snake. "Madam Fangs to you, and I am not a mouse."

"Hello, Madam Fangs," murmured Bright Eyes, wondering how to get rid of this unwanted visitor.

"I think I'll stay a while," said Madam Fangs haughtily, slithering in a little further, completely blocking the entrance to the burrow.

"Whiskers will be home soon," Bright Eyes quivered.

"How nice," Madam Fangs' smile became even wider. "He'll be just in time for lunch!" She reared up. Her eyes, glowing like a pair of pale moons, seemed to fill the room. Bright Eyes shivered, unable to move or speak. Then with a loud swish Madam Fangs swooped down on Bright Eyes and swallowed her whole. Bright Eyes kicked and struggled, but she was inside the snake, and the more she struggled, the deeper she slid down a horrible black tunnel that was squeezing the life out of her.

At that moment Whiskers was happily trotting home when he noticed something black and glistening protruding from his burrow. Tiny gold lights darted off it as it writhed and flicked.

Whiskers' blood ran cold. He dropped the food he was carrying and ran as fast as his legs would carry him toward the burrow. "Bright Eyes! Bright Eyes!" he cried. But all he could see was the end of the snake's tail turning and flicking. The snake was obviously smacking itself on the ground, forcing something down that it had just swallowed. Whiskers leaped on the tail and sank his teeth into it.

Madam Fangs squealed as a shaft of pain traveled from the tip of her tail up her slender body and exploded in her head. She was being attacked from outside, while inside, the mouse was putting up a fight that really startled her. In a panic, she tried to pull her tail in, while her attacker was trying to drag her out.

"It must be the other mouse," thought Madam Fangs. "I'll fix his wheels."

She whirled around only to realize that Bright Eyes made such a bulge in her body that she could no longer get through the narrow opening. Nor could she free her tail from her attacker's grip. Aside from the excruciating pain, her attacker was tearing off the lovely scales she was so proud of. She had to get out of there somehow, she thought desperately.

With tooth and nail, Whiskers tore the scales off the snake's tail and sank his teeth into the flesh. Madam Fangs was shaken by a great spasm of pain. Her jaws flew open, and Bright Eyes plopped out. Madam Fangs gazed at her prey dully. She opened her jaws to swallow the mouse again, but something else was attacking her now. The Rooster, seeing Whiskers' brave efforts, had joined the fray, pecking at the snake's tail with all his might. Madam Fangs was really alarmed, for her attackers were dragging her out of the burrow.

Whiskers darted past her to comfort Bright Eyes, who was dazed and bedraggled but none the worse for wear. Madam Fangs, however, found herself gazing into the Rooster's angry red face.

"It was a mistake," she tried to explain, glancing at her damaged tail out of the corner of her eye. "I'll be on my way now." She tried to sidle away, but the Rooster shook his head menacingly, blocking her way. The hens, who were never far from him, closed ranks behind him.

"Oh dear! Oh dear!" thought Madam Fangs. "What a pickle I'm in!"

Running feet were approaching, and the chickens drew back. Madam Fangs breathed a sigh of relief, which quickly turned to horror. A very large human loomed over her with a broomstick raised ready to strike.

"Don't harm it," she heard a soft, musical human voice say.

"Oh, all right!" grumbled the large one. "Just the same, I don't like snakes. Particularly not in your garden."

With a swipe of his broom, the Pet sent Madam Fangs flying through the garden gate to land with a loud plop in a muddy ditch on the other side of the road. The snake lay quite still until the world around her stopped spinning. Nervously, Madam Fangs looked about. She was filthy and smelly. Her beautiful tail, not to mention her pride, was in tatters.

"Nobody must see me in this state," she told herself. When she was sure nobody was watching, she slinked away.

"Oh, Whiskers," hiccuped Bright Eyes, "I was ever so frightened."

"I can't leave you a moment without you getting into trouble," scolded Whiskers, trying to sound stern, but really relieved that Bright Eyes was safe.

"Oh, Whiskers," said Bright Eyes after a while. "I don't like it here anymore. Can we go back to our old place?"

"After all my trouble!" cried Whiskers. "I thought you wanted sunlight and fresh air and flowers and all that!"

"Please, Whiskers," begged Bright Eyes. "I promise to be careful . . . I promise . . ."

Whiskers grinned and stroked his mustaches. "I'll think about it. I'll think about it," he said.

THE
FISHER'S TALE

Wang Fu had fished the same stretch of the Li River all his life. After an unusually long wet season a dozen years ago, the river changed course. The fish stock dropped so alarmingly that most of the fishers moved with the river while others took up another trade. Wang Fu did neither.

"You are so stupid and stubborn!" his wife complained. Wang Fu nodded dully. The best way of shutting her up, he discovered, was agreeing with her. But his wife was in no mood to be put off.

"Liu San is learning to be a carpenter," his wife dinned in his ear. "But you! You're shiftless. Why don't you go further downstream instead of trying to catch fish where there aren't any!"

That was not true. Wang Fu would not go on fishing the same stretch of river if there weren't any fish. It was merely that their numbers had dwindled. Also, Wang Fu was careful not to take more than he needed to support his wife and himself. Neither did he keep young fish that would mature and propagate their own kind. Thus, he eked out a frugal living. However, he had not caught a thing five nights in a row.

"Oh, what a trial this man is!" wailed Wang Fu's wife, rolling her eyes to heaven. "We shall starve!"

"It will be better tonight," mumbled Wang Fu.

"Better!" That word set his wife off again. Wang Fu's wife did a quick sum in her head. She had carefully secreted a few strings of coins under a loose brick in her kang (a sleeping platform), but that was for her old age. If Wang Fu's luck did not change, they would be in real difficulties! She ranted till she was quite red in the face, then flapping her arms like a disgruntled hen, retreated to her kitchen to vent her spleen on the pots and pans.

At dusk Wang Fu pulled on his cape woven out of reeds, gathered up the bundle of food his wife prepared for him, and headed for the river. On his way he stopped at the wine shop and bought a small jar of rice wine.

Wang Fu kept his bamboo raft lashed to an old sycamore that leaned over a large, flat rock on a sandbar in a sheltered elbow of the river. Once the river teemed with rafts, and the light of flaming torches bounced merrily off the rippling black surface of the water as night fell. Now only the wind in the trees, the rush of the river, and the cry of an occasional night bird broke the silence. He missed the laughter and the easy camaraderie with the other fishers, but his roots were here, and he was loath to leave it.

He lit a fire beside the flat rock. After he had made his raft and net ready, Wang Fu placed a small dish of food on the flat rock and sprinkled some wine around it. Then he clapped his hands thrice and banged his forehead three times on the ground.

"Oh, River God, accept these unworthy offerings," he prayed, "they are all I have. Bless my labors this night. I do not ask for more than enough to keep body and spirit together. Have mercy, O River God."

He got on his raft and poled it to the middle of the river. Shifting his weight from side to side, he nosed the craft into the current, which carried it toward the next bend in the river. There he lit a torch fixed to the raft's prow and cast his net. Sometimes he did not have to wait long for the fish to rise. That night, like the five nights before, his net filled with weeds that grew beneath the surface of the water. He poled the raft back to his camp with a heavy heart. Patiently he picked off the weeds and lay them out on the rock to dry beside the fire. They would eat waterweeds the next day, he thought grimly. Then he went back to the river to try again. Close to dawn Wang Fu returned exhausted but empty-handed. He tossed a handful of twigs on the embers of his fire and settled down to munch his food. It is cold in the hours before daybreak. Wang Fu was grateful for his reed cape and the jar of wine to help ward off the growing feeling of despair. Had there not been a moon he might not have noticed a man gliding soundlessly through the underbrush. It's probably a traveler, thought Wang Fu as he snuggled into his reed cape waiting for sleep.

A few nights later he saw the man again, sitting on a log near his camp. Wang Fu could tell by his long, flowing robe that he was a gentleman. With little imagination and no curiosity, Wang Fu quickly lost interest. That night he had cast his net twice, and twice pulled in nothing but weeds. All he could think about was cleaning his net and setting out again.

Nevertheless, Wang Fu felt the man's gaze on his back as he worked, and it made him uneasy.

"Excuse me if I don't stop to chat," he said without turning around. "A man has to make a living, and I'm not having much luck tonight."

As he carefully plucked the weeds tangled in his net, he wondered whether he had somehow offended the River God. Perhaps his offerings were too meager for what he took from the river. That thought sent a quiver of dismay rippling through him. What would become of him if the River God refused him fish? The river was not only his livelihood, it allowed him to be his own man. Wang Fu could not bear the thought of living like poor Liu San, who couldn't call his soul his own since he apprenticed himself to a carpenter.

"There are fish in the river, if you go about it the right way," a voice cut across his thoughts. Wang Fu dropped his net and peered into the dark. The firelight was in his eyes, and all he could make out were the tips of a pair of thick-soled shoes. Wang Fu leaped to his feet.

"What . . . what . . ." he stammered.

"I startled you," the stranger smiled reassuringly. "I think I might be able to help."

Wang Fu started to say something, but the other gently cut him off. "Let me explain."

At close range the man looked older than Wang Fu had thought. Indeed, his gown was longer than gentlemen of his class wore nowadays.

With the tip of his finger the stranger traced a curved line in the sand.

"Let's say this is the river," he began. "We are here," he made an X to mark the place, "and this is where the fish are." He pointed at another spot, pausing while his last remark sank in. "You must go to the fish because they won't come to you."

Wang Fu's chin dropped to his chest. He had never been farther down the river than the next bend. "But they've always come up here!" Wang Fu insisted, doggedly staring at the crude map in the sand.

"They won't any more," said the gentleman with certainty.

"Why?" Wang Fu searched the other's face.

"Maybe they're bored. Fish need to be treated as intelligent creatures too," was the reply.

Wang Fu never doubted the intelligence of fish. Sometimes he was not sure of his own.

"Take me on the river, and I will show you," said the gentleman with a wink.

"I can't do that," Wang Fu muttered, and his shoulders sagged. "Couldn't you just tell me what to do?"

Fixing Wang Fu with a piercing gaze, the other quickly stripped down to a loin cloth. "Now we are equal," he chortled. "Come!"

There was nothing for Wang Fu to do except scramble after him. The stranger untied the raft and poled it expertly into the stream, as familiar with the river as if he had been born to it. He knew where every rock, tree stump, or root lay treacherously under the surface, ready to shred the flimsy craft. The river narrowed. Its murmur became an excited babble. They skimmed along faster and faster. Wang Fu clung to the edges of the raft until his knuckles were white and numb, his teeth chattering with fright. He had never been this far down the river before. The stranger, however, shifted his weight easily with each swell, laughing up at the star-speckled sky. It seemed an eternity before the river broadened, becoming peaceful again. The stranger unlashed the paddles tied to the sides.

"We'll row a little ways," he said, "then you light the torch and cast your net."

Being told what to do did not sit well with Wang Fu. Nevertheless, something about the stranger's tone compelled him to do as he was told. Presently the stranger put up his paddle. They had come to a place where Wang Fu could not touch bottom with his pole.

"Cast when I tell you," said the stranger. Next moment, he slipped off the raft and disappeared into the shiny, black water. All the blood rushed to Wang Fu's head. What if he drowned! Just as Wang Fu decided to flee that place, the stranger's head broke the surface a few hundred yards ahead.

"Cast!" he shouted.

Wang Fu obeyed as if in a trance. The stranger disappeared again. Suddenly the water in front of the raft was churning as fish raced toward the spot where he had cast his net. In a great sweat, Wang Fu began hauling it in, arms, legs, and back straining against the weight, heart pumping so hard that he thought it would pop out of his chest. Finally the net was secured, and the river was calm. In the excitement, he had forgotten his companion. With wildly trembling hands Wang Fu trimmed his torch and waved it this way and that, anxiously probing the dark. There was no sign of the man. The thought that he might have drowned set Wang Fu's teeth chattering again. He wanted to leave that dark stretch of river, but somehow he could not move. Just then a rustle of movement made him turn to the shore. There, at the river's edge, stood the stranger.

With a great effort Wang Fu found his voice and shouted, "Hey! Hey! I thought you drowned!"

The other replied with a clear, ringing laugh.

"Wait! I'll come in for you!" cried Wang Fu, reaching for a paddle.

"No !" the stranger called back as he slipped into the trees beyond.

"Hey!" shouted Wang Fu, "Wait!"

"Go back!" came the reply.

"I haven't even thanked you!"cried Wang Fu, but the stranger had already vanished.

That night's haul was the biggest and the best of Wang Fu's entire life.

The next night before he went down to the river, he demanded a few extra coins from his wife for some good wine for the River God.

"River God!" scoffed his wife. "It's my prayers to the Kitchen God that turned things round." For once, Wang Fu stood up to his wife.

"I earned the money," he reminded her, "and I'm going to spend some of it the way I choose!" The look on his face so startled the wife that she gave Wang Fu the coins he demanded.

"You make sure the River God gets the wine," she yelled after him.

That night after he had made his offering to the River God and prepared to set out, the stranger came strolling by.

"Hey!" shouted Wang Fu, flapping his arms to attract his attention.

"Hey!" the stranger waved back, "I've come to fish with you."

The stranger took charge as he did the night before. Again they came back with a good haul. Afterward, as the two sat by the fire to rest, Wang Fu shyly unwrapped his meager bundle of food.

"It's only fresh leeks and pancakes," he said, "but my woman always puts sesame oil in her pancakes."

The stranger tore off a chunk and chewed it with obvious enjoyment. Wang Fu poured some wine into a bowl and handed it to him.

"No, thank you," the stranger demured, though his eyes brimmed with longing.

"Don't stand on ceremony," insisted Wang Fu. "There's enough for the two of us."

"No thank you," the stranger replied with infinite sadness.

Wang Fu was abashed.

"I . . . I . . . was . . . only trying to be friendly," he muttered miserably. "You've been so helpful driving the fish into my net . . . and . . . I have no way to thank you . . ."

The stranger clapped him on the shoulder.

"I had fun!" he chortled. "That's enough."

From then on Wang Fu and the stranger fished together. It never occurred to Wang Fu to ask his name or where he lived, nor was it volunteered. The stranger would not touch any part of the money Wang Fu made.

"I have no need for money," the stranger said, "but I will ask two favors. You must never tell anyone about me, or where you fish."

Wang Fu nodded.

Months passed. One night when they met by the river, the stranger seemed preoccupied, not his usual ebullient self. Wang Fu was concerned.

"Maybe you shouldn't go on the river tonight," he suggested.

"Nonsense," the other responded. "A bit of exercise will do me good."

However, he was moodily silent all the way down the river to their usual destination.

"You haven't told anyone about this place, have you?" the stranger suddenly asked.

"No!" exclaimed Wang Fu, eyes wide.

For the moment the stranger busied himself making fast the raft. Then, turning, he said, "Wang Fu, you drive tonight and I'll cast."

Wang Fu had wanted to try his hand at driving the fish for some time but never had the courage to suggest it. Now he leaped at the chance.

"Why, I'll be glad to!" he cried, but something in the stranger's face—or was it a trick of flickering torchlight—gave Wang Fu pause. He shook it out of his head, filled his lungs with air, and dived into the water. He went down the way the stranger told him. His weightless body glided easily through the black silence, guided by the light of the torch, glowing like a dozen fractured moons high above. He moved in rhythm with a strange music that seemed to swell around him, pulling him ever deeper until he became one with the river. His movements became slower and slower until they stopped. Calmly he watched air bubbles rising slowly to the surface. A joy so complete engulfed him that all he wanted was to sit at the bottom of the river, surrounded by the music of the deep. Slimy green weeds stealthily creeping up his legs shocked him out of his revery. Frantically he tore at them, but the harder he tugged, the stronger the weeds kept him anchored. He tried to scream for help, but he had no voice. The lights dancing high above flickered and went out.

Wang Fu came to, face down on the familiar sandbar. A strong pair of hands kneading his shoulders and back made him retch until he was empty.

"Thank you for saving my life," Wang Fu gasped, instinctively knowing it was the stranger leaning over him. "I am . . . even more . . . in your . . . debt . . ."

"Don't be too hasty to thank me," said the stranger.

With a great effort Wang Fu turned over to gape blankly at his friend.

"You will understand, presently." The stranger's shoulders sagged with weariness. He covered Wang Fu with his reed cape, and threw a handful of sticks onto the fire.

"Once there was a young daredevil," the stranger's voice sounded strangely hollow. "He wasn't a bad person. Just high-spirited and thoughtless. He liked wine more than he should, and when he was in his cups did silly things. That year the rains didn't stop when they should. The river was rising, ready to flood. He should have been helping the townsfolk pile sandbags along the bank. Instead, this young man was in a tavern playing drinking games with his friends. They were all quite drunk," the stranger sighed ruefully. "By that time, the river was cresting. Someone suggested going down to watch it flood. One of the group offered to give a feast for anyone who dared cross the river by an old wooden bridge that stood swaying over the raging waters. The young man, who was always game for a dare, scrambled onto it. Before he was halfway across, the pilings gave way, sending the bridge crashing down. The young man was swept into the Underworld. The Lord of Shades would not accept him before his time, so he sent the young man to the River God. The River God felt vaguely responsible, but the young man had not completed his life's tasks. Neither had he fulfilled his obligations nor realized his potential in the world of the living. Consequently, the River God condemned him to wander until he could lure someone to a watery death to take his place . . ." The stranger fell silent. The two men faced each other without a word. Wang Fu was the first to break the silence with a shudder of recognition.

"How long has it been?" he asked.

"A century is a blink of an eye," replied the other. "Being stuck between two worlds is terrible, so I had to find a substitute . . ."

confessed the stranger. "I watched you a long time, before I went to work. First I kept the fish away. Then I pretended to be your friend. Finally I tricked you into diving . . ."

"I don't have much to live for," muttered Wang Fu recalling that moment of rapture at the bottom of the river. "Why did you bring me back?"

"You trusted me, gave me the unconditional friendship that I never experienced before in your world . . ." said the stranger. "That's why I couldn't let you die. Rest. I will trouble you no more."

With that, he vanished into the night. Wang Fu slept without dreams. At dawn he woke, and having given thanks to the River God for his bounty, trudged off to market with his haul. At the end of the morning, he went home with his empty baskets slung on his back. As usual his wife was waiting at the door with her hand out. As usual he dropped his purse in it without a word.

Wang Fu's life did not change visibly, yet nothing was the same. For a short time he had a friend who shared his labor and his simple food. Now that friend was gone, and Wang Fu was the poorer for it. He fished, alone as he used to. Often he thought of the deep pool the stranger showed him. He longed for its inviting indigo darkness. Most of all he yearned for the strange, haunting music and the wonderful lightness of being. Since he could not bring himself to go there, he went back to the meager catches he hauled in from his familiar stretch of river.

"You lazy, good-for-nothing!" his wife badgered. "If I were a man, I would show you a thing or two!"

"Maybe you can, anyway," Wang Fu snapped back. "I could have . . ."

"Could have what?" shouted the wife, arms folded across her chest.

His wife's scorn drove him back to the deep pool.

Wang Fu fastened his raft to the stump of a half-submerged tree jutting out of the water. He did not light the torch. Darkness enveloped him in its velvety embrace. The river lapped invitingly against the raft. Weariness and fear fell away. Peace was only inches from the tips of his toes. A voice hailed him just as he was about to slip into the dark water.

"Hey! Is that you?" cried Wang Fu excitedly.

"Who else?" the stranger guffawed out of the dark.

"I've missed you!" Wang Fu shouted, quickly lighting his torch. "Come closer, so I can see you."

"You can only see me if you leave your world," laughed the stranger. "The River God made me Guardian of the river because I couldn't let you die."

"I'm ready," retorted Wang Fu vehemently. "There is nothing to keep me here."

"Remember what happens to those who leave before their time?" the stranger warned. "You must find the strength to endure."

Wang Fu gulped, his eyes suddenly misting.

"Stay where you belong," the stranger's voice rose from the river. "Each full moon, I will fish with you . . . Go now . . ."

"How will I know you if I can't see you?" Wang Fu spoke to the river. His own voice bounced back out of the dark. Nothing more.

They say on nights of the full moon a dust devil would come whirling down the riverbank, and Wang Fu would follow it on his raft wherever it led. When he came ashore before sunrise his baskets would be brimming. Wang Fu's Dust Devil's catches soon became a local legend. When he was buried, a dust devil appeared over the grave and was seen skipping merrily down the river. Near the place where there is believed to be a deep pool, it disappeared.

THE
NIGHT SINGER

A stiff wind whipped the fine spring rain into swirling bluish gray mist. The barge appeared like a mirage behind the grunts and shouts of the boatmen on the towpath, dragging her up Chien Tang River. I knew it was Master Tang Hao the moment I set eyes on him, standing alone on the prow. He was a tall, spare man. A writing case slung over one shoulder made an ungainly bulge under his long, gray cloak. A pathetic bundle of belongings lay at his feet. As I picked my way down the slippery embankment to the quay, the barge dropped anchor, and passengers swarmed ashore. For a moment I lost sight of my master's guest. I found him at the edge of the dock, deep in thought. I hurried over to him, babbling a welcome speech on behalf of my Master that I had memorized the night before.

"I have a carriage waiting," I pointed up the embankment, and snatching the bundle from his hand, quickly proceeded up the slope. Master Tang squished along behind me. Finally, we were settled in the carriage and the driver urged the horse into a lazy clip-clop.

My Master's annual instructions concerning his various properties in Hangzhou arrived as usual on the second day of the new year. He is a meticulous man who leaves nothing to chance. As estate agent, I was expected to execute his orders precisely, and report twice a year. Otherwise, my reclusive Master did not wish to be disturbed. I had worked for him almost a decade, but it was the first time that the villa on West Lake was mentioned.

". . . You are to reopen Lakeside Villa. Make it livable by the first day of the third month," my Master wrote. "However, the east wing of the main courtyard must remain sealed. Master Tang Hao, a scholarly gentleman, who is recovering from a lengthy illness, will take up residence there for an unspecified duration. He requires rest and tranquility. You are to engage a reliable servant to see to his comfort. Lay in provisions in keeping with hospitality, without being extravagant . . ." He gave detailed instructions as to which of his accounts kept with local merchant houses were to be used. "I leave everything to your discretion," he concluded. "Master Tang has the run of the villa with the exception of the aforementioned east wing." The last sentence was written in bold characters for emphasis.

I stole a glance at Master Tang Hao. In answer to my solicitude, he murmured a few words, whose inflection betrayed the fact he was not a native of our province and probably learned our dialect out of necessity. The brevity of his response showed he did not wish conversation, so we rode in silence.

Lao Liu, the general factotum I hired to oversee Master Tang's needs, had lit a brazier in the main room. Pine cones and needles laid over glowing coals filled the air with a resinous warmth. Having shown Master Tang his quarters, I left, promising to return in a day or two. However, he was to send Lao Liu to me if he required anything at all.

In all the years I have served him, I have never met my Master or any of his clan. The family had been prominent merchants of

Hangzhou for generations, until they suddenly quit the city a dozen years ago. Rumors were rife at the time but died after a while, as they generally do. My Master, who inherited the family fortune soon after, lived in the capital. The others scattered to the four winds. None ever returned. Although Lakeside Villa is listed on the register of my Master's holdings, he never mentioned it. Since he did not tolerate questions, I did not inquire.

Opening the villa, however, proved to be more difficult than I expected. Roof and windows had to be repaired or replaced. A coat of paint was required inside and out. Rooms had to be aired. Furniture cleaned and made serviceable. Finding men willing to work there was a problem.

"Unspeakable things were done in that house," the elder of a nearby village growled at me balefully. "Evil never dies."

"What are you talking about!" I bristled.

"Ask your master," the old man rubbed his hands together as though he were washing them and stalked away.

In spite of fear and superstition, I hired a crew by offering outrageous wages. However, nothing would induce workers to stay the moment the shadows lengthened in the afternoon. Nevertheless, the job was done according to my Master's wishes. I persuaded Lao Liu, who cooked for the work crew, to stay on. He went from town to town picking up whatever work he could, and the job meant a roof over his head and three squares a day for as long as Master Tang stayed.

A week or ten days passed before I visited the villa again. I found its tenant dozing in the courtyard. Even in sleep he looked haggard. The fine bones of nose and cheeks were almost visible under the pasty, translucent skin. The eyes were sunken and black rimmed. The only touch of color was in the full-lipped mouth. The long-fingered hands folded on his lap were thick-veined, strong, and callused, unlike the soft, ineffectual hands of a scholar. His clothes, though well kept, were years out of fashion. Round his neck he wore an amber amulet carved in the shape of dragon and phoenix entwined. There was something oddly poignant about that ornament, for half was missing. The state of his shoes showed he walked more often than he rode. Master Tang was probably another failed candidate of the Imperial Civil Service Examinations, in search of a patron. My Master had a soft spot for genteel vagrants.

Master Tang snapped awake, instantly alert. He greeted me without rising. Nor did he offer me the empty chair. After the usual pleasantries, I asked if his quarters were satisfactory.

"Yes, yes," he replied with a wave of the hand. "Except one thing."

Then he told me about the night singer.

"Night singer?" I echoed.

"I hear her late at night," explained Master Tang Hao, "from over there."

I followed his gaze to the sealed east wing that looked forlorn in contrast to the rest of the courtyard. Nothing had been done to it since it was not to be used.

"You must have heard a nocturnal bird," I said, reeling off the names of a few common night-warblers.

"One that also plays the lute," Master Tang shot back sarcastically.

"Or, you might have . . . "

". . . Dreamed it," Master Tang snatched the words right out of my mouth. "That might have been the case before . . . but I'm much better now . . . much better . . ."

I leaped at the opening to broach the question that was uppermost in my mind.

"What was the matter?" I asked, weighing my words with sympathy.

Master Tang Hao dismissed the question with an impatient gesture.

Taking another tack I asked, "Does the singing disturb you?"

There was a faraway look on his face when he said, "A woman singing, accompanying herself on the lute is very . . . soothing . . ."

I was sufficiently intrigued to bring it up with Lao Liu.

"Night singer!" croaked Lao Liu in his curious raspy voice, "Why, he accused me of getting drunk and singing late at night! His nibs apologized later." He tapped his temple and winked significantly.

"Were you drinking?" I asked, for I smelled cheap liquor on his breath.

"Just a tiny drop," he rasped. "This place gives me the creeps. But I swear on my ancestors' bones, there isn't any 'Night Singer.' If there was, I would have heard it, wouldn't I?"

I decided the night singer was nothing more than a figment of Master Tang's imagination.

A few days later Lao Liu came to me in great excitement. That afternoon I rode out to the villa. Master Tang Hao had broken into the east wing. I found the double doors had been pried open, and roughly secured again with a piece of firewood thrust through the looped door handles.

Master Tang Hao, who was writing in the main room, waved me into a chair, while his brush glided in a swift, continuous movement down the page. When he looked up I was struck by the change in him. The black circles round the eyes were gone, and so was the haunted look in their depths.

"It's a new poem! I've found my muse again!" he crowed, obviously pleased with himself.

I dragged my mind back to the reason for my visit and stated my business as solemnly as I could. Master Tang heard me out with an amused smile.

Realizing I was not making an impression, I blustered, "I shall have to inspect the rooms, and ascertain . . ."

Next moment, Master Tang was dragging me to the east wing.

As he flung the door open, the rancid smell of disuse smote me in the face. Part of what must have been an antechamber had been crudely walled up, leaving a long, narrow space, bare except for a ruined scroll hanging on the facing wall. It would appear a mischievous child had gone over it with ink and brush. However, the black swirls that covered it had such vitality, it seemed to throb with life. I was mesmerized; lost in a tangle of black tentacles that seemed to reach out for me.

"The Night Singer is in there," Master Tang whispered in my ear. His hand made wild swirling motions in the air. "Those brambles imprison her . . ." I blinked hard to rid myself of the tangled black lines that weaved and danced before my eyes. I stumbled out of the room, leaving Master Tang gazing fixedly at the scroll, humming a tune under his breath. For a moment in that stuffy room I was taken in. However, in the light of day, I knew it was just a ruined painting that conjured up strange ideas in a diseased mind. I feared Master Tang was mad. I must make him leave before he does any real damage, I thought. A handful of coins persuaded Lao Liu to keep an eye on our guest and to report anything out of the ordinary. A few days later Lao Liu came to me with a note. Master Tang Hao requested me to purchase five or six exotic herbs, a clay pot, and several calligraphy brushes of various sizes.

"It is imperative I have these materials as soon as possible," he wrote.

I had to scour the apothecary shops and the stationers of Hangzhou to assemble everything on the list. However, a particularly fine brush Master Tang asked for eluded me. Fate must have guided me to a dingy stationer's shop in the old part of town.

"I might have such a brush somewhere," the shopkeeper murmured, surveying his unkempt premises. He bustled about, opening and shutting cupboards, foraging in mysterious drawers, clucking, and muttering to himself.

"I used to bring in this type of brush for a particular customer . . ." said he from behind a partition where I could hear him moving boxes. "A talented young lady who wrote and sang poetry in Soong dynasty style. She wasn't rich, but this is the only type of brush she used. She had such a fine hand that I sometimes let her pay with pieces of calligraphy . . ." Presently he emerged with a slender box lined with silk on which was nestled a brush whose reddish horse hair tip was fashioned into a bulb ending in a needle-fine point.

"The lady who ordered it was called Xiaoyu—Jade of the Dawn," he prattled. "She was a lovely little thing! Her father sold her as a concubine to the oldest son of a wealthy merchant . . ." He shook his head and sighed.

The next afternoon I went to the villa with my purchases. Lao Liu greeted me like a fellow conspirator.

"He's in the east wing," he whispered.

I found Master Tang Hao seated cross-legged on the floor, gazing at the ruined scroll. At first he was oblivious of me, then, with a shudder, he came to.

"Have you got the things?" he cried without preliminaries. I handed over my parcel. He unwrapped it, muttering "yes . . . yes . . ." at each item. His excitement gave me goose pimples.

When he had examined everything, he smiled, and it seemed a shaft of sunlight touched his face. "My lady will be pleased," he breathed.

My ears pricked up. My Master had given run of the villa to him but to no one else. This may be my excuse to rid myself of my Master's peculiar guest.

"Who is the lady?" I asked.

"Lady Xiaoyu, who sings to me in the night," replied Master Tang with a strange gleam in his eye. That moment we seemed to inhabit different spheres. It was the second time I heard that name in as many days. Was it coincidence, or had I stumbled onto something beyond my ken?

An inexplicable curiosity compelled me to examine some old ledgers the previous estate agent had left me. I kept turning pages until I came upon the words "Lakeside Villa." The entry, dated a dozen years earlier, showed bricks, mortar, plaster, whitewash, and tools had been purchased for work done on the east wing. However, there was no record of artisans' wages. Instead, half a dozen male servants were given sizeable stipends and sent to the family's holdings in distant provinces a few days later. A winding sheet was also purchased without a coffin. Indeed, there was no mention of a funeral. During the same period horses, wagons, and several carriages were acquired, consistent with the family uprooting itself soon after. There the accounts for the villa ended.

Sixth sense drove me back to the villa. It was after nightfall. Lao Liu opened the gate, waved me in the direction of the east wing and scurried for the kitchen, hands clapped over his ears. I followed him.

"What's going on?" I hissed shaking him by the shoulder.

"Don't you hear her singing?" whimpered Lao Liu, a wild look on his face.

All I heard was the wind in the trees and the soft lapping of the lake against the shore.

"It's driving me mad!" groaned Lao Liu. "I won't stay any longer!" Between chattering teeth he told me how Master Tang Hao had brewed his herbs and applied the liquid to the mysterious painting.

"Slowly those brambles, or whatever he calls them, melted away," Lao Liu's tone was filled with wonder. "Then I heard her singing . . ."

The door and windows of the east wing were wide open, and the light of the waxing moon flooded the room. Master Tang Hao sat before the scroll; an ecstatic smile lit his face. The black lines that obliterated the painting were gone, except for a few tenacious tendrils clinging to the corners. An ethereal young woman gazed out of it, lips slightly parted as if about to sing. One slender hand cradled a lute while the other plucked its strings. In the uncertain light I thought the artist had painted something that appeared to be a fragment of a charm hanging from her neck. Though I had never seen the portrait before, the feeling of recognition made me shudder. I seemed to hear the lady's voice, barely audible, but warm and insistent. My inner self strained after her words.

"You hear her too," breathed Master Tang Hao without moving.

His words jolted me back to reality. Even as I denied anything of the sort, I felt the eyes in the portrait fixed upon me. The lady's voice sounding in my brain filled me with exquisite pain. Master Tang Hao's eyes were on fire when he added, "She will be free when the moon is full!"

I felt I was drowning. With a huge effort I propelled myself out of the room and fled.

That night I rooted through my Master's papers. In a bundle of correspondence bearing his father's seal were a number of letters from Wang Xin, a marriage broker, concerning the acquisition of a concubine for my Master. The young lady in question was the beautiful and talented daughter of a cultured family who had fallen on hard times. There was an impediment. The girl had already been promised to another. However, the father, who was in desperate straits, was willing to overlook certain niceties for a price.

Negotiations dragged on. The Old Master doted on his son. So gifts of money, silks, jewels, and even a small house were made to one

Wu Tiansiang as a marriage portion for his daughter Xiaoyu. There it was again! Xiaoyu! I was delving into matters I instinctively felt should be left alone, yet I was powerless to desist.

Wu Tiansiang's house was not hard to find, but the family had moved away a long time ago.

"He fancied himself a gentleman, with all the airs and graces," a neighbor who spoke to me sneered. "But he sold his daughter to the highest bidder. They say the girl tried to escape the rich man's villa on the lake with her betrothed. Something went wrong . . ." He paused. I slipped him a few coins and he continued.

"The young man hired a boat for the night, which he would row himself. There's nothing unusual about that, except the boat was found capsized the next morning and there was no sign of the young man. There was gossip he had been killed."

"Wasn't there an inquiry?" I asked.

"What for?" the man answered my question with one of his own. "They say he was from out of province, one of hundreds who came for the civil service examinations. Without money or connections who would bother! Nevertheless, the rich man pulled up stakes soon afterward. Then Wu Tiansiang quietly sold his house and left too."

I seemed to have reached a dead end.

I thought of the marriage broker. Wang Xin had also gone from the place where he used to live. The family was reticent. However, when I mentioned my Master's name, a gleam of interest flashed in the eyes of a nephew.

"My uncle has lived in a monastery for the last ten years," he volunteered.

A few coins and he supplied its name. The look in the man's eyes told me nothing more was forthcoming.

Master Wang Xin was one of several old men who lived in the monastery and did menial tasks in exchange for food, shelter, tranquility, and a decent burial when he dies.

The monk who pointed him out working in the garden said, "We believe he is possessed. By day he is silent, but he sings at night. Always the same tune." He murmured a blessing and withdrew.

Master Wang Xin's face was as wrinkled and dry as a prune. At first he showed neither interest nor surprise at my presence. Suddenly something flickered behind those opaque black eyes.

Out of the blue he said, "He couldn't win Xiaoyu's heart, so he had her portrait painted to enslave her soul." He leaned close to me and whispered, "That night he was supposed to be away, and the other was coming for her in a boat." For a moment his attention wandered. Then he added, "Only he never got there." Wang Xin grabbed me by the collar and hissed in my face, "He was killed!"

"By whom?" I stammered.

"The one you work for," he said quite distinctly. "The girl's father got wind of the plan and told me, and I told your master. I needed money!" His face crumpled into a grotesque mass of crisscrossed lines. "He walled her up alive in his ancestral shrine. Then he destroyed her portrait so that her soul will never rest in peace . . ." Wang Xin's eyes went blank. He had forgotten me.

It was a long ride back to the city. I stopped for a jug of wine to calm my nerves. It was dark when I left the tavern. The flower-scented night was pleasant, and I was in no hurry. As I clopped along, the full moon rose. Between the trees a sliver of West Lake gleamed in the distance. Suddenly Master Tang Hao's mysterious remark came back to me. I dug my heels into the horse and galloped toward the lake.

The villa was completely dark, but the gate was open. I shouted for Lao Liu. There was no answer. The door to the kitchen had been torn from its hinges. Inside, smashed furniture and utensils were strewn about, evidence of a fierce fight. The struggle had clearly continued across the courtyard, for I stumbled over a sleeve torn from a cotton tunic like the one Lao Liu wore. I ran to the east wing.

A peculiar stain, like the shadow of another person defaced Xiaoyu's portrait. A sickening smell of decay came from a hole smashed through the facing wall. I covered my nose and mouth and peered through the opening. Inside was a crumbling ancestral shrine. Shreds of a linen winding sheet and a lute lay in the dust. What else I glimpsed has been blotted from my mind.

Sounds of movement outside startled me but no one was there. I sprinted out the gate and down the path to the lake. Master Tang Hao was poling a skiff away from the shore. A veiled woman sat in its prow. I started to call out to them, but my voice froze in my throat. The woman turned, and as she lifted her veil a cloud drifted across the moon, plunging us in momentary darkness. When it passed, the lake shimmered smooth as glass.

The following morning an overturned boat was found floating on the lake. Nearby, tangled in weeds at the bottom were the skeletons of a man and woman locked in eternal embrace. They crumbled into dust when they were brought to the surface. Each wore half of an amber pendant.

I closed the villa, and my Master accepted my explanation for Tang Hao's departure without comment.

I thought things would be the way they used to be, but that is not the case.

In the dark hour before dawn, I hear a raspy, faraway voice singing a tune imbedded deep in my consciousness. Every note pushes me closer to the edge. There is no escape. I will have to go back to Lakeside Villa.

But not today.

Not today . . .

M'Lady

❦

*L*i Shu leaned back in his chair and tilted his face to the sun streaming through a high window. Behind his tight shut lids, molten globes of light sent rivulets of warmth coursing through his frame. He shuddered as knots of tension in bone and muscle began to unravel. Little sounds filtered through his drowsing brain, detached and far away. For the moment he was at peace.

Lady Chan, seated at her desk across the room, glanced up from the pile of bills and invoices she was scrutinizing as her husband shifted position. A shadow of concern passed briefly across her face. Satisfied that he was comfortable, she returned to her work. The gallery where she sat afforded a clear view of the bustling general store below, while an ornate screen hid her from those she observed. It was widely known, though never publicly acknowledged, that Lady Chan not only ruled Li Shu's household but ran his business as well. For Li Shu was a clever but indolent young man who would have run it into the ground. Since his marriage five years ago, his wife brought order if not purpose into Li Shu's life. Under her stewardship, the business prospered. Lady

79

Chan prided herself on knowing who her customers were and anticipating their needs. Furthermore, she knew her staff. A new broom sweeps clean. She quickly weeded out the flatterers and the panderers who buzzed around her husband like bluebottle flies around a honey pot and sent them packing. The rest she won over with her sincerity, her fairness, and her acumen. Her husband had to admit she ran the business better than he ever could.

Hovering between sleeping and waking, a pair of almond-shaped eyes, upward tilted at the corners, floated to the surface of Li Shu's consciousness. Like a reflection in water they beckoned, remote yet tantalizing. He sighed. His wife across the room looked up again. Lady Chan knew her husband well. The trouble with Li Shu was that he was unfocused. He took the Imperial Civil Servants' Examination but failed to distinguish himself. Then he tried painting, for which he had shown some promise. His doting parents had given him a studio in a quiet lane on the other side of town and stocked it with everything an artist needed. For a time, Li Shu went there every day, but he did not produce anything worthwhile. Most of the time was frittered away in the company of other would-be artists and poets, waiting for a bolt of inspiration to strike. When Lady Chan married him, she knew full well she was not sought after for her beauty or the size of her dowry. It was the qualities she possessed, which Li Shu lacked, that made her the ideal mate for the heir to the family business. She married without illusions, but she was captivated by Li Shu's beauty and easy-going charm and soon came to love him passionately.

Often when Nanny was combing her hair at bedtime, Lady Chan would ask, "Nanny, have I been a good wife?"

The old servant, who had come with her as a bride, pursed her lips and murmured something inaudible.

"Nanny?"

"Just keep asking," the old woman replied, not missing a stroke.

Lady Chan was asking herself that same question now, but never with more uncertainty. Ever since the last rent day a month ago, she sensed a change in Li Shu. He was usually home from the country by nightfall. That time he did not return until the following morning, weary and out of sorts. When she inquired where he had been, he was short with her for the first time in their married life.

"A man has the right to spend time with friends without having to account for every moment!" he shouted.

The rent money he turned over to her was short.

"I spent some," he said.

"On what, honored husband?" she pressed.

"This and that!" he flayed the air with his arms. "It doesn't matter."

"Oh, but it does," she countered. "The rent money belongs to the business."

"The business! The business!" he cried. "Can you think of nothing else? What about me?"

Those last words reverberated in her mind. In her zeal for her husband's financial well-being, had she lost sight of the man? That thought sent waves of dismay through her. She kept a well-ordered and comfortable home. She was attentive about Li Shu's likes and dislikes. She thought she had left no stone unturned where her husband's happiness was concerned. Evidently something was amiss. She would ask Nanny where she had gone wrong. Nanny always had an answer.

For once Nanny had no ready answer. If she did, she was reticent.

"Nanny!" Lady Chan's tone took on an impatient edge. The two women's eyes locked in the dressing table mirror. Nanny gave her mistress's long, glossy hair a tug before she applied her comb to it again.

"Nanny," Lady Chan softened. The old woman's mouth was pursed into a tight knot. It was a look that Lady Chan knew from childhood. Nanny would speak when she was good and ready. Lady

Chan studied her own reflection as she waited. Hers was not an unpleasant face, but somewhat flat. Everything about it was round; the single-lidded eyes set too close together; the curved arches of the painted brows; the small, snub nose. In contrast with the rest, the wide, thin-lipped mouth seemed out of place. However, with her hair worn loose, her face did not seem quite as broad and plain. Surreptitiously, she essayed a smile, hoping Nanny would not notice. But the old woman obviously did, for she gave her hair another tug and leaning close to her mistress's ear whispered, "He has a person living in the studio."

Lady Chan's hands flew to her throat. The color drained from her cheeks one moment, and blazed the next. Nanny went on combing.

With an effort Lady Chan asked Nanny's reflection, "What person?"

"A female person," replied Nanny testily. "Young and quite pretty . . ."

Lady Chan whirled about and seized Nanny's hand.

"How do you know?"

"I followed him," said Nanny. To justify herself she added, "He has been acting strangely ever since he came back from the country last rent day."

Her husband had indeed been behaving strangely. He was lethargic all day but seemed filled with feverish restlessness when the sun went down. He slipped out of the house as soon as the evening meal was over and did not crawl into bed until almost daybreak. He slept badly, grinding his teeth and muttering. Once or twice Lady Chan thought she heard him murmur in his sleep, "M'lady . . . M'lady . . ." She was touched, thinking he was dreaming of her. Now she wasn't sure.

Lady Chan examined her husband's face from across the room. He did not look well. Come to think of it, he had not looked well since she discovered the two tiny punctures on his neck.

"It's nothing," Li Shu had reassured her. "Probably some insect bite." Nevertheless, he quickly pulled up his collar to hide them. As he slept with his head turned to one side exposing his neck, she could see quite plainly the punctures had not healed. In fact they were oozing, the flesh around them purplish and bruised.

Another sigh from the sleeper snapped Lady Chan out of her reverie. She cleared her throat just loud enough to wake Li Shu. He came to, dazed and disoriented.

"You were dreaming, honored husband," Lady Chan smiled with her lips, but her eyes quickly registered Li Shu's discomfiture. He mumbled something as he rearranged his robe, shifted his body in his chair, ready to doze again.

"Honored husband, the parchment you ordered has arrived," she said, holding up the bill.

Li Shu's eyes snapped wide. He knew Lady Chan was waiting for him to say something, but he didn't trust his voice.

"I would have ordered it for you, if you told me," there was an unmistakable note of reproach in Lady Chan's tone. "I will have it sent to the studio," she added.

"There's no need," Li Shu said quickly. "I will attend to it myself."

"One of the delivery boys can take it."

"I said I will attend to it myself!" Li Shu cut her short.

Their glances clashed. Li Shu was the first to look away.

"It's a present for a friend," he explained.

It was the opening she had been waiting for.

"Who is she?" asked Lady Chan.

His stricken look cut her to the quick. Li Shu ran his hand wearily across his face. There was a feeling of relief, now that the moment he had been dreading was upon him.

It was Indian summer and hot the day he rode out to the country to collect his rent. Li Shu was a city dweller for whom the countryside held no enchantment. The landscape behind a scrim of yellow dust was monotonous. The people were dirty and uncouth, always whining about their appalling living conditions, which he could do nothing about. His Steward used to do this chore until Lady Chan dismissed him because some of the rent money stuck to his pockets. Li Shu would have overlooked it, but Lady Chan had to make an example of the poor fellow. From then on rent collecting became his responsibility.

"A monthly excursion to the country would be a pleasant change, honored husband," Lady Chan was always reasonable. "Besides, a landlord must keep track, or those peasants will cheat him blind." As usual he could not fault her. Nevertheless, trips to the country were not his idea of a pleasant pastime, and he made sure his wife was aware of it.

"I shall have a special dinner prepared for you when you return," she said to mollify him, reeling off a list of his favorite foods.

It would have been the same uneventful trip as usual if his horse hadn't lost a shoe on the way home. The village smithy had to be cajoled out of the tavern in the midst of a boisterous drinking game, to restart the fire and shoe the animal. Li Shu swallowed a few bowls of raw sorghum wine while he waited, which put him in a somnolent mood. Matching its master's humor, the horse ambled on at an easy pace, till, with a start, Li Shu noticed the shadows had grown long and the sun was rapidly dipping toward the horizon. The city gates would close for the night and he would be shut out if he didn't hurry. He urged the horse into a gallop. As he rounded a bend, a figure muffled in a long, black cloak darted across his path. The horse shied and would have thrown a less skillful rider. As it was, it took all Li Shu's strength and willpower to bring it to heel.

"Are you hurt, idiot?" Li Shu shouted angrily as he circled back. A quivering mound of black cloth lay on the road, whimpering.

The horse rolled its eyes and snorted, as the cloaked figure struggled to its feet.

"Are you hurt?" bellowed Li Shu. "I have no time to lose!"

The figure stood before him quivering without a word.

"Let's have a look at you." With the tip of his whip Li Shu flicked aside the hood that hid the other's face. A pair of enormous almond-shaped eyes, tilted upward at the corners gazed up at him. The face, framed by glossy black hair, seemed to glow in the fading light. It was a face that he had never seen before, yet somehow he knew its every line. It was the most beautiful face he could ever hope to find. But it was the eyes that mesmerized him, that drew him into a whirlpool of unaccustomed emotions to which he abandoned himself without any scruples.

"Where are you going, unattended, so late in the day?" he asked gently.

The girl's lips parted as if to speak, but didn't. Instead, the eyes suddenly brimmed.

"Please don't cry," Li Shu stammered. "I didn't mean to be harsh back there . . . Are you hurt?"

"I'm all right," she murmured, burrowing into her cloak so that only her eyes showed. "Please go."

"I can't leave you here," he glanced quickly at the empty expanse around them. "The countryside is full of brigands. You'll never reach the city gates before they close."

"I'll be all right," said the girl from behind the folds of her cloak, fighting the quaver in her voice.

On an impulse, Li Shu reached down and swept her onto the saddle before him and spurred his horse into a gallop. She cried out and struggled at first. But he held her fast. Suddenly the fight went out of her, and she nestled against him like a captive bird. They rode in silence. Everything passed before Li Shu's eyes in a blur. A curious scent like bitter almonds sent the blood roaring through his veins.

Every fiber in his body was singing. Never had he felt so alive. Instinct took him to the studio.

"And that is all?" Lady Chan asked equably. Li Shu nodded, but the look on his face was like a knife thrust through her heart.

That night was a flashing kaleidoscope of sensations and emotions in which Li Shu drowned, died, and was reborn. Nervously he adjusted his collar to hide the two little punctures that were the marks of indescribable ecstasy. Through the ringing in his ears he heard Lady Chan say, "Since this person is essential to my honored husband's happiness, she should be brought into the household. I shall make arrangements today."

"You mustn't," cried Li Shu. "She does not wish to be a part of anyone's household. She is like a . . . like a . . ." he fumbled for words.

"She is a butterfly that cannot be caged?" suggested Lady Chan.

She was so small, delicate, and beautiful that all Li Shu wanted was to hold her and protect her from whatever it was that made her take flight.

"I will stay if that is your wish," she had said with surprising resiliency and strength when they spoke of the future the morning after. "However, nothing in your life must change."

Li Shu started to protest, saying the studio was not a suitable place to live in. She countered by saying she would turn it into a place where he could take his ease whenever he wished. Besides, she was also an artist. Indeed, the pathetic bundle of clothes she carried also contained an ancient box of paints and brushes.

"They are the only things I value from the past," she murmured.

She would not hear of formalizing their relationship. "I must be free," she said fixing Li Shu with her eyes. "Otherwise I shall die." She came from a background of genteel poverty. Her father had sold her as a bride to the local warlord, known for his capricious cruelty. However, before she was delivered to her lord and master, she had escaped.

"So, she is a runaway," sighed Lady Chan, "and betrothed to the warlord, no less." She waved aside her husband's rebuttal. "We all know he is a monster, but do you realize the consequences of what you have done? When he finds her . . . and he will . . . he will kill the lot of us. Including your revered parents," she added for emphasis. "What is her name?" Lady Chan was suddenly businesslike.

"I don't know," mumbled Li Shu reddening.

It was the truth. When he asked her name, she replied, "The name I was born with is dishonored. The one I am destined to bear, I despise. Therefore, I have no name."

"What shall I call you?" he whispered, cupping her face between his hands.

"Whatever you wish," she said. He thought a moment.

"I shall call you . . . M'lady . . ." He repeated it several times, rolling it off his tongue with infinite tenderness.

She laughed, and it was like the tinkling of a little silver bell.

Lady Chan stiffened. Her worst fear was confirmed. Her husband was smitten with the girl. But her voice was calm when she spoke again.

"For all our safety, she must leave the studio. Hide her where she can't be traced back to you."

"I will think about it," said Li Shu without much conviction. Inwardly he knew he would do nothing for the time being, no matter the consequences. For he noticed that M'lady had grown wan and listless.

"It's being cooped up," she said with a languid smile. "I wish I could walk about the streets in broad daylight like any ordinary person!"

"But you can!" cried Li Shu. "I shall accompany you, and no one will dare harm you. I promise!"

She shook her head. "That will put you in danger. I couldn't bear it if harm came to you. I must go away . . ."

Li Shu's heart lurched within him at those last words. Frantically he cast about for something to relieve her boredom. He smacked his forehead, when he looked about him.

"You could paint here!" he cried. Eagerly he flung open cupboards and drawers to show her their contents. "Everything you need is here!" he cried. "Use them!"

"I have," she countered. "It's only a poor effort." Shyly she produced a small ink and brush sketch of Li Shu.

He complimented her for the likeness, but when he begged to have it she refused. "I did it for myself. That way a little of you remains with me when you are absent," she said. Seeing his crestfallen look she added, "I will do one of myself before I go."

"You must not speak of leaving," cried Li Shu.

"But go I shall," she replied, stroking his cheek with her thin, birdlike hand. "It's inevitable. When I am gone the portrait will remind you of me." Then taking a more cheerful tack, she asked him to buy her some parchment, as fine as human skin, for her portrait. She smiled, and the tiny greenish lights dancing in the depths of her eyes dazzled him so that he had to shut his own. A red mist engulfed him that left him chilled to the bone, weary, and disoriented when it receded. He remembered vaguely writing an order for the parchment before stumbling to his living quarters in a courtyard behind the shop. The rest was a blank.

Now that the parchment had arrived, Li Shu chafed to deliver it, but M'lady had insisted he must not alter his daily routine on her account and that he was not to go to the studio until after dark.

"If you love me as you say, then you will abide by this simple request," she said earnestly.

"Why?" cried Li Shu.

She tweaked his nose and chuckled. "Because it's best for all of us," she said.

So he waited till dark before he hurried to the studio with the roll of parchment under his arm. M'lady was pathetically grateful for his gift. She unrolled it carefully on the long table used for painting, examining it carefully inch by inch. Her breath came in short, sharp gasps, and the finger tip that glided down its length trembled with excitement. That evening M'lady was more animated than she had ever been, darting about the room, chattering all the while. Yet in the flickering candlelight, Li Shu was startled at how changed she was. She looked haggard. He thought he detected the beginning of lines across her forehead and around her eyes that he had not noticed before. Nothing she said penetrated, until suddenly he found himself in the street with the gate locked in his face. A flash of annoyance faded to disappointment, then to resignation. He leaned his head wearily against the jamb. His feet seemed too heavy to lift, his legs too wobbly to carry him away from there. By and by when he was himself again, he trudged home. The streets were empty. The shops all shuttered and most of the houses dark. He was aware time had passed, but he had no recollection how. Only M'lady's parting words stayed with him.

"You must not come here until I send for you," she said. "I must be left alone a while to paint."

"How long will it take?" he cried.

"Art takes time," M'lady smiled.

Li Shu did as he was bid. He stayed away from the studio though he seethed with impatience. Lady Chan watched his misery helplessly. He was by turns irascible then apologetic for his rudeness. He seemed to shrink before her eyes until he was a shadow of himself. In spite of the terrible fatigue, Li Shu roamed the streets aimlessly. Lady Chan did not try to stop him, but she had Nanny dogging his footsteps at a safe distance. Li Shu receded into himself. A transparent veil separated him from the rest of the world. Thus, he was dazed and bewildered when a pair of hands suddenly shot out from the throng in the street and slammed him against a wall. The back of his head striking a hard surface shocked him back to reality. Li Shu found himself staring into the angry face of a mendicant monk.

"You are bewitched!" thundered the monk, white whiskers bristling and spittle flying in all directions. "An aura of evil surrounds you! You are damned!"

Li Shu stared at his attacker, too overcome to speak. The monk seized the collar of his robe and pulled it down. To the crowd that gathered around them, the monk said in a quieter voice, "Just as I thought. The evil one has been draining your blood." He pointed at the two festering wounds on Li Shu's neck. The crowd let out an audible gasp and backed away. "I have pursued this evil creature for a long time . . ." The monk pressed his face close to Li Shu's and whispered urgently into his ear.

Li Shu shuddered. His mouth opened and shut like a fish out of water.

"You're mad!" he finally croaked, struggling free from the monk. The monk's face was grim, but he did not try to detain Li Shu.

"You have the choice between life and death, but you choose death. So be it." He sauntered down the street, leaving Li Shu clinging to the wall for support, gasping for air. Had he been alert he might have noticed his wife's Nanny hurrying after the monk.

Li Shu could hear his own heart beating as he hurried toward the studio at a half-trot, propelled by what he had just heard. The gate was bolted from within as he expected. He went around to the back where part of the wall had crumbled, which he had meant to repair but never did. Breathless with excitement, he squeezed himself through the breach into the small courtyard at the back of the studio. On hands and knees he crept up to the window. There was a faint sound of movement within. Once or twice he thought he heard someone gibbering and chuckling. He wet a fingertip with spittle and applied it to the rice paper that covered the window, working it gently until there was a hole to peer through. What he saw made his blood curdle. Dizzily he scrambled through the hole in the wall again, hailed a carriage for hire, and headed home.

Li Shu's teeth were chattering when Lady Chan helped him into bed. He clung to her, wild-eyed with terror. Lady Chan made him comfortable with her usual quiet efficiency.

"There, there," she soothed, stroking Li Shu's feverish forehead, "you've caught a chill wandering the streets without a cloak in this weather."

Lady Chan's presence was a comfort. She was constant, unchanging no matter what happened. He clutched her hand in both his. "Help me!" he gasped, "I'm afraid!"

"Of what, honored husband?" cooed Lady Chan. "You're home, lying in your own bed."

He wanted to tell his wife about the monk; then he caught sight of Nanny standing behind her with a bowl of something hot in her hands, and he stopped. He did not like Nanny. Worse than that, he did not trust the woman. He would wait till they were alone. In the meantime, he allowed himself to be propped up with pillows, and Lady Chan spooned a brackish, brown liquid into him.

"The nastier it tastes, the more effective it is," said Lady Chan, as though she were coaxing a child. Li Shu tried to respond, but his tongue was so numb it would not form the words. He lay back and shut his eyes. He dozed. Once more he was peering through the tear in the window screen of the studio, hungry for truth. His heart refused to believe that the hag with the stringy hair and burning eyes he saw drooling over a painting spread out on the long table was M'lady. It had to be an impostor in her clothes, for M'lady is young and beautiful.

"You live because she needs you," the monk's implacable voice sounded again in his ear. "From time to time she must rejuvenate herself by painting a portrait of herself on parchment, which will become her new skin. But to go on living she must also have a new heart. She will take yours when it suits her . . . Then you will join her as a creature neither dead nor alive, but forever damned. Lead me to her while there is still time!"

Li Shu thrashed about in his delirium. He tried to cry out, "She is not an ancient vampire," but he could not. The monk faded into a gray void. Li Shu sighed. Suddenly his clothes felt so tight he had to struggle out of them. Free at last, he stood beside the bed, light and insubstantial, gazing down without surprise at his other self lying there. Lady Chan was slumped in a chair nearby, eyes shut. He followed the path of a pearl-like tear trickling down her cheek unheeded. When he tried to brush it away, he found he could not. Nor did she hear when he called her name. He moved with the long loping strides of an antelope. A sensation that filled him with childish delight. He did not have to open the door. He simply went through it. Once outside, he bounded lightly across rooftops, his shouts of joy rang to the skies.

"M'lady! M'lady!"

The cry from his heart found an echo. She came to him with the greenish flecks dancing in her eyes, and eagerly he surrendered to the red mist that enveloped him.

A force, stronger than anything he had ever experienced, suddenly reeled him back, and he lay once more in his bed. A painful weight pressed down on his chest so that he could hardly breathe. Through slitted eyes he took in the room flooded with daylight. He sensed there were people about, though they were beyond his field of vision. The fire door of the potbellied stove in the center of the room must have been open, for his nostrils twitched at the smell of burning paper. Presently it clicked shut.

"I hope that's the last of her letters."

Li Shu recognized his wife's voice, but his head was so heavy he could not shift it to see who she was addressing.

"Surely she must realize by now that he will not go to her," Lady Chan continued. "A sensible person would leave."

"Ah, need I remind you, dear lady, she is not," a man's voice held low, answered. The voice sent ripples of fear through him. With an effort he made a sound that was half groan and half bleat. A finger pried open one eye. At the same time a hand grasped his wrist firmly but gently. In that instant Li Shu recognized the monk.

"Is he coming to?" asked Lady Chan. "He looks as though life is draining out of him."

"Perhaps it is, dear lady," whispered the monk as he released Li Shu's wrist, "in spite of our efforts."

"But these . . . things . . ." cried Lady Chan, "were supposed to keep her at bay!"

Li Shu forced his eyes open a crack wider. Bunches of herbs festooned his bed. Now he understood where the strange pungent smell wafting through the air was coming from. Instinctively, he knew it had something to do with M'lady. He would have torn them down if he had the strength.

"They will stop her for a while," the monk responded. "Right now she communes with his spirit," he paused as if to forestall something Lady Chan was about to say. "We can control the body but not the spirit. The creature will become desperate, for her new skin will wither without a new heart."

That last remark filled Li Shu with loathing for the speaker. He had to admit M'lady puzzled him. For instance, she had quickly ferreted out his favorite foods and prepared them for him, but she never partook. Nor would she allow him in the house till nightfall. There had to be a logical explanation, if only he had the strength to pursue it.

Lady Chan let out a low groan. "I've heard her pacing and whimpering in the courtyard at night."

"Ah!" there was a note of triumph in the monk's voice, "we are drawing her out . . ."

Li Shu was sure now some diabolical plot was being hatched against M'lady while he lay helpless. He must warn her somehow. Li Shu stirred. The monk's hand seized his wrist again.

"Our sleeper wakes," he whispered.

Lady Chan's plain, round face blocked out everything else. Li Shu hadn't the strength to refuse the brown, brackish liquid she fed him. Presently she laid him back, and he drifted off. The shadows were stretched long across the courtyard when Lady Chan emerged from Li Shu's chamber with Nanny close on her heels. Muffled in long cloaks, the two slipped out of the house, walking briskly toward the city gate.

"Oh, my pet, let me go instead. It's no place for a lady," pleaded Nanny.

Lady Chan never flinched from anything unpleasant she had to do.

"No!" she shot back. "It's a matter of life and death for my husband. It concerns no one else but me. Let us press on!"

Nanny glared at her mistress's back balefully, knowing better than to contradict her. Once through the city gate, they turned onto a dirt road that branched off the main highway. Even before they reached it they could smell the garbage dump. Fumes writhed from it, gyrating in a mocking dance in the afternoon sun.

"Wait here," Lady Chan commanded the disgruntled Nanny over her shoulder.

Fighting down waves of nausea, Lady Chan scrambled up the hillock of rotting matter. Inwardly she railed against the monk for having sent her on this mission.

She would have turned back except for the monk's challenging words reverberating in her mind. "I can be of no further help, but one wiser than I can. Ultimately, only you can conquer this ancient evil," said the monk. "It will take all the strength you can muster. Most of all, it requires limitless and unconditional love."

The look he gave her made her quake. She gritted her teeth and swore she would do whatever he commanded, "Even at the cost of my life!" she cried.

Clawing her way up the slippery, shifting side of the hillock, a stubborn streak that would not let her admit defeat drove her on. Lady Chan wondered dully if pride alone was enough to conquer this wretched hill? With every step she sank deeper into the slime. Already she had lost her shoes to the evil smelling muck. Now her petticoats and robe, saturated with moisture, weighed her down. She lost her footing, pitched forward and slid down the slope. She picked herself up, dazed and blinded momentarily by the low-lying sun, and started again. Sweat mixed with tears of desperation and humiliation bathed her cheeks.

A barking laugh from somewhere high above her jerked Lady Chan's face in that direction. Shading her eyes against the sun, she saw a grotesque figure perched on the top of the hillock, more like a gigantic spider than a human being. Her heart missed a beat, but she fought the quaver in her voice and called out, "I seek the Holy Hermit."

The creature leaped in the air, did a wild jig, and chortled mockingly, "She seeks the Holy Hermit!" Coming to a stand still, he added in a high-pitched squeal, "Doesn't everyone?"

Lady Chan swallowed hard, for as her eyes grew accustomed to the light she could see the man was as filthy as his surroundings and probably mad. She drew a deep breath and asked, "Are you the Holy Hermit?"

"Who else might I be in this hallowed place?" the man shot back. "Come closer that I might see you!"

Lady Chan looked dubiously at the way ahead, and her heart sank. A mocking laugh from above made her clench her teeth. She hoisted up her skirts and bare legged, attacked the slimy slope again. The human spider watched her, laughing, shouting insults and encouragement between snatches of weird incantations barked at the indifferent heavens.

Lady Chan fell again. Her hair, which had come undone, was a mass of sticky tendrils that fell across her face, blurring her vision. Indeed, her face was so covered with grime that only the whites of her eyes showed. She struggled on blindly, step by painful step, her heart fluttering like a captive bird in her chest. At times earth and sky seemed to change places. Then the light was in her eyes and the wind upon her face.

"So!" cried the Holy Hermit from beneath his thatch of stiff, grime-spiked hair. "What do you seek?" Then, adopting a teasing manner, he answered his own question. "Methinks you have come to marry me!"

Lady Chan felt her cheeks burning. Before she could let loose an angry retort, the Holy Man leaped to his feet and closed the distance between them in one bound. He took her chin in one hand and jerked her face to the light.

"Not pretty," he pronounced letting his hand drop. "No matter. I am not the marrying kind."

"I am already married," stammered Lady Chan.

"More is the pity," returned the Hermit, "for the husband."

Hot tears scalded Lady Chan's eyes. She fought them back, determined not to give this rude creature the satisfaction of seeing her cry.

"Well, what is your errand?" shouted the Hermit. He seized her by a handful of hair and dragged her to the edge of the slope. "If you have no errand be gone!"

Lady Chan twisted free. The shifting slime underfoot brought her crashing down upon her knees. The last vestiges of pride shattered. In great wrenching sobs she told her story.

The Hermit listened, dancing a jig and shouting wild incantations all the while. Then turning serious at the end of Lady Chan's recitation, he said in an almost gentle voice, "Gather me some white fungus, and some black."

"Where will I find them?" hiccuped Lady Chan.

The Hermit seized her by the hair again and dragged her around the top of the hillock, pointing here and there, shouting, "Look! Hither and yon! Here and there! Everywhere!"

He let go of her abruptly, plopped himself down and, assuming the lotus position, was completely still. Neither tears nor entreaties could move him to utter another word. The sun was rapidly racing toward the horizon. Lady Chan got down on hands and knees, foraging in the filth for the fungus. To her amazement, she found them growing from the rankest filth, gleaming with a strange iridescent beauty. She tore off a strip of her petticoat to hold them.

"A dozen of each will do," said the Hermit as if he spoke to the wind. "Then go!"

"But what shall I do with them?" Lady Chan quavered.

"You will think of something," the Hermit muttered. His head fell forward, and he began to snore.

Lady Chan stood shaking with exasperation. She would have stamped her feet in rage if the mush were not slowly sucking her under. The Hermit was sound asleep, and daylight was waning fast.

Nanny cried out in dismay when her mistress stumbled off the noisome hillock clutching her cache of fungus. Lady Chan found Nanny's horror unaccountably amusing. Filthy and barefooted, she felt liberated. Without a word, she strode purposefully toward the city gate, head held high. It was Nanny who slinked behind hiding her face in shame.

Bathed and dressed in fresh clothes, Lady Chan examined her precious handful of fungi. The white ones were shaped like clusters of stars, while the black ones were curled and corrugated like cock's combs. Away from their natural habitat they emitted a sweetish, faintly steamy smell. In fact she found it rather soothing. She sent Nanny to the temple to ask the monk what she was supposed to do with them, but he had gone away. However, the Hermit had said she would think of something. She sat down beside her husband's sickbed to ponder that. Gazing at Li Shu's ashen cheeks, she fancied she saw him laid out in his coffin. Perhaps the fungus was an elixir to break M'lady's spell. Once that idea took root, Lady Chan flew into action. She set a kettle of water on the potbellied stove to boil and dropped the fungi into it. They hissed when they hit the water, quickly turning into a gelatinous mass that dissolved. Soon a sweet, heady perfume that made Lady Chan's head spin filled the room. She shut her eyes, and was instantly asleep.

There must be a windstorm, thought Li Shu, for the rattling of the window brought him out of a deep sleep. By the light of the guttering candles he could see something was cooking on the stove. Another odor, stronger than the herbs that festooned the room, tickled his nostrils and made his eyes water. His wife stirred in her chair. She too had been wakened by a noise.

A scratching sound came from the window. A nocturnal bird must be pecking at the rice paper thought Li Shu. Then his eyes went wide with fright. He could hear someone breathing outside. The window paper broke with a loud tearing noise. A woman's hand reached in, groping for the latch, encountered a bunch of herbs fastened to it, and drew back with a cry of surprise and pain. Sweat beaded Li Shu's brow. He tried to heave himself out of the bed, but something held him down. He could not move, nor did he have the strength to cry out. Whoever it was hovered outside muttering, pacing rapidly up and down. Suddenly, the window burst open, and a disheveled woman climbed through it giggling and gibbering. The candles had gone out. Li Shu could not see the woman's face, but recognized the scent of bitter almonds.

"M'lady! M'lady . . ." he gasped.

"I have come for you, Li Shu," she replied in a voice that dripped honey. "Why have you abandoned me?"

Li Shu tried to answer, but his wooden tongue would not shape the words.

She approached the bed cautiously, uttering irritated sounds at the bunches of herbs that barred her way.

"Come to me," she pleaded stretching out her arms. "You promised me your heart, but you are false like all men!"

Li Shu shook his head feebly.

M'lady's arms dropped to her sides. Her body coiled like a cat's and she leaped upon the bed, bringing down bunches of the herbs as she landed. For a moment an invisible web seemed to fall upon her, causing her to cry out. Lady Chan shot to her feet. In the dark she could barely make out a figure straddling her husband, one hand clutched around his throat, the other tearing at his nightshirt. Blind with terror Lady Chan reached for the pot simmering on the stove. Distracted by the movement, the crouching figure turned, whereupon Lady Chan flung the contents of the pot in M'lady's face.

M'lady's piercing shrieks were horrible to hear. When the sound subsided, Nanny crept into the room. She found it in shambles. The air was foul with the acrid smell of something burning. Her master and mistress were in a dead faint but apparently unharmed. No one else was there.

Months passed before Li Shu fully recovered from his mysterious illness. Neither he nor Lady Chan ever mentioned the events of that night or M'lady. They blocked it from their minds. It was as though nothing had happened.

A year later Lady Chan persuaded Li Shu to sell the studio. He did not object since he never used it. However, before showing it to a prospective buyer, Li Shu decided to visit the place, to be sure there was nothing he wanted to keep. He found a roll of parchment tied with a red ribbon. He recognized the clumsy double knot with which it was tied at once. His own handiwork stirred memories. He threw it in the fire with the rest of the rubbish without looking at it.

The truth is Li Shu was no longer sure M'lady ever existed. Nor could he conjure up the face that was once so dear, except the upward tilting eyes, black as the night, with curious green flecks flickering in their depths. However, two tiny scars remained on his neck for the rest of his life.

THE
BUTTERFLY

*A*t the age of thirty, Ning had already failed the Imperial Civil Service Examination twice. His father, who wanted him in the family business, did not encourage a third attempt.

"We have been tea growers for generations," coaxed the Father. "That continuity must not be interrupted by whim!"

"Surely, the Ancestors would be just as honored if I were a Minister, or the local Magistrate!" Ning argued.

In the end his Father gave in to Ning's wheedling, but not without conditions.

"You must swear before the Ancients," said the Father with a deep frown, "if you do not succeed, you will settle into the family business, marry, and produce offspring to carry on the family name."

Ning grudgingly took the oath.

This time he passed the preliminary examination and was summoned to the provincial capital to write his final thesis. Ning was elated, con vinced it was a sign the Ancients were on his side. He arrived at Hangzhou in a buoyant mood and tramped the city from one end to the other seeking lodgings. Every square inch of space was taken. Footsore and dispirited, he was in despair. Maybe the Ancients were trifling with him, bringing him so close to his goal, only to thwart him. How could he write the thesis that would make his fortune without a place to live? He was drowning his troubles in a tavern when he overheard a conversation about an abandoned house in the hills overlooking Chien Tang River. Ning decided to find it. He lost his way several times, but persistence eventually paid off.

The house was almost in ruin. Beyond the entrance courtyard was another with rooms built facing each other on the east and west sides. A slip of paper with the words "KEEP OUT" inked on it was pasted to the door of the one facing east. So Ning took the other.

Ning settled in. From time to time he glimpsed a shadowy figure moving in or out of the room facing his. Whoever it was chose to stay aloof, which suited him. He was glad of a roof over his head and solitude to write his thesis. For the first few days he struggled fruitlessly. On a grim, rainy day he suddenly tapped into a wellspring of inspiration that seemed endless. The steady drumming of rain on the roof merged with the stream of thoughts that spilled from the well-formed tip of Ning's brush. Later in the day the rain stopped. Silence severed the thread of concentration. Ning stretched, easing the ache in his shoulders. He was thirsty. Reaching for a bucket, he headed out to the well.

The garden beyond the courtyard had gone to seed long ago. Weeds and brambles obscured everything except a path to the well that seemed to have been trampled through the rough growth quite recently.

The well stood at the edge of a terrace that had partly crumbled away. The rope fastened to the rusty winch was worn but serviceable. As he bent down to draw water, a movement at the corner of his eye made Ning look up. A butterfly gently opening and folding its mottled wings of gold and purple, perched on the cobblestones, poised for flight. Ning watched it lift into the air, gliding and dipping around him as though observing him from every angle. Suddenly it veered away and disappeared into a dense grove of green-black pines that screened the lower half of the garden from view.

The butterfly's departure left Ning strangely bereft. He tried to settle down to his thesis again, but he could not pick up where he left off. There was a strange fluttering in his breast, as though a butterfly were imprisoned there. He could not sit still. The squeaking of a rusty hinge across the courtyard was an excuse to lay down his brush. He opened his door just as the occupant of the room across was about to go in.

He was a grim-faced man. Deep-etched lines from the corners of his eyes to the curve of his chin gave him a sardonic look. The haughty, aquiline nose and the wide, thin-lipped mouth added a dash of brooding remoteness. The long, lank hair pulled back and tied with a ribbon at the nape of the neck, the tunic, pants, and thick-soled boots he wore were in keeping with a man of action.

Ning introduced himself eagerly.

"No doubt you are writing the Imperial Examination," the stranger said in a surprisingly cultivated accent.

Ning babbled when he was nervous. The other hushed him with an impatient gesture.

"Have a bowl of wine with me, an hour hence." The invitation sounded more like a command. "An hour hence," repeated the stranger as he shut his door firmly in Ning's face.

"Who does he think he is!" thought Ning angrily. He resolved to stay away. Soon the smell of cooking wafted through his window. What is wine without food! Ning's rumbling stomach overcame his pique. He splashed some water on his face, ran a comb through his hair, changed into a fresh robe, and crossed the courtyard precisely an hour later.

The stranger's room was identical to Ning's, except it was festooned with bunches of herbs whose various aromas mingled dizzily in the air. Charms to ward off evil spirits, written in a bold, fluid hand, covered the walls. A dilapidated bench stood to one side heaped with scrolls. Several appeared to be charts of the constellations. The only object not covered in dust was a sword in a leather scabbard hanging over the kang.

The two men sat crossed-legged on the kang with food and wine laid out between them. Ning's host had not introduced himself earlier, nor did he trouble to do so now. Conversation came in short, disjointed spurts, as it usually does between strangers. When they had polished off the plain but hearty fare and a passable wine, the silences became tedious. Ning was tempted to make his excuses and leave. However, too much wine and the overlapping perfumes of herbs fogged his brain. Everything blurred.

Ning woke with a throbbing head. It was dark and raining again. He fumbled in the dark until his hand encountered a candle, which took real concentration to light. The evening was a jumble of ambiguous impressions, bits of which flashed sharp and clear in his mind.

He lay back trying to piece together what he could remember about his neighbor. "He's too old to be seeking a position in the civil service," Ning muttered to himself. Since he had been living in this lonely place, he had started talking to himself. "He could be a necromancer . . ." The charts in his room seemed to point in that direction. Ning brushed that notion aside when he remembered the sword hanging on the wall. "He's a paladin!" he said out loud. That did not add up either, for the man carried himself like a gentleman. "So where does that leave us?" Ning answered his own question, "Nowhere."

Ning remembered only one remark from their conversation. His host had warned him not to venture out of his room after dark.

Ning had laughingly asked why.

"For your own good," was the answer repeated several times.

Ning could have kicked himself for not pursuing the subject. No matter. He had no intention of venturing out into the dark, wet night. He snuggled into his quilt and prepared to go back to sleep.

A scratching sound outside the door gradually insinuated itself into his consciousness.

"Who is there?" Ning called out. The sound stopped. As Ning lay back it started again.

"Is someone there?" Ning called again, his throat oddly dry. The sound stopped again. Ning heaved himself off the kang, and flung the door open.

A girl stood on the threshold, her tiny frame drooping with weariness. Rainwater trickled off her hair and down her heart-shaped face. Her almond eyes, fringed with long, graceful lashes, brimmed with fear. Ning softened instantly.

"Come in," he said gently. She sidled past him, eyes demurely averted. The guttering candle filled the room with darting shadows.

"Please sit," Ning said, indicating the kang where he slept, ate, and worked. "As you can see, I don't have much." Noticing a faintly condescending smile cross the girl's face, he added, "This is only temporary." His nervousness made her giggle.

"You'll be an official at court one day," the girl said.

"You're laughing at me again," Ning blurted, and instantly felt foolish.

"Not at all," said the girl, who could not have been more than seventeen or eighteen. "I can tell by the curve of your brow, the arch of your nose, the shape of your mouth," her gesture encompassed Ning's person, "your bearing . . ."

Ning chuckled all aquiver. He loved flattery.

"I shall light the brazier and make tea," he stammered, busying himself.

The girl seated herself on the edge of the kang, her tiny feet barely touching the ground. She had removed her wet traveling cloak. Under it she wore a robe of pale yellow silk splashed with purple flowers befitting a lady of rank. However, at that moment, she was more like a wet butterfly, spreading her wings out to dry.

Ning had the brazier lit and the tea kettle humming in a trice.

The girl prattled merrily. She said she was on her way to her grandmother's and got caught in the rain.

"Lightning frightened the poor horse and it bolted. I'm a good equestrian," she said emphatically. "Anyway, I am safe now." She sipped her tea, smiling at Ning with her eyes.

They talked desultorily for a while.

"I am so weary," said the girl, eyeing Ning's rumpled quilt. "May I sleep here?"

Ning was thunderstruck.

"That's impossible," he blustered, his arms flapping in agitation.

The girl's tinkling laugh made him bristle.

What do I know about her? he asked himself. Suppose she is a great lady! In that case, her mere presence would spell doom not only for him but his entire family and their servants too.

"Woe betide me!" Ning groaned in spite of himself.

"And all because I want to spend the night in your room!"

The derisive gleam in the girl's eyes convinced Ning she was making fun of him.

"My lady had better leave," he muttered stiffly.

"Leave!" the girl's eyes went wide, "just when I was getting comfortable!"

Ning picked up her cloak, which he had spread on the floor near the brazier to dry, and held it out to her, his eyes fixed to the ground. He knew that if he looked at her his resolve would crumble. She had to go!

"Perhaps a little something will change your mind," the girl murmured. From the folds of her robe she drew a silk purse and jingled it under Ning's nose. "Now, can I stay?"

Ning gulped, and shook his head.

The girl returned the purse to its hiding place, snatched the cloak from Ning's hands, and headed for the door.

She stopped on the threshold, one hand on the latch.

"Look at me," she commanded. "I want you to look at me." She stamped her foot.

Ning hung his head

"You are a hard man," sighed the girl. "Maybe that's why I like you."

A gust of wind blew out the candle as she let herself out.

An elusive but distracting fragrance remained in the room after she was gone. The mysterious young girl who briefly had intruded upon his solitude created a disturbance he had never experienced before.

In the days that followed, Ning forced himself to write, but he produced only words without art or content. The thought of coming so close to his goal and having it slip through his fingers filled him with self-loathing.

The stranger also seemed restless. He practised with his sword long, strenuous hours, until the weapon became an extension of the man. He ignored Ning, as though they had never met. However, one evening as he was going to his room, he said loud enough to be heard, "The path of righteousness is narrow, fraught with danger. Be watchful . . ."

Ning was about to ask what he meant, but the stranger had shut his door.

Later, as he struggled with his thesis, the girl stole into his room, smiling with her eyes. The gush of words that rose from his heart, died on his trembling lips. Ning watched transfixed as she dipped a new brush in water to soften its bristles, rinsed his stone, and ground fresh ink. When the ink was ready, and she had tested the point of the brush for the correct softness, she placed the implements before him on the rough planks laid across bricks that served as a writing surface.

"Write," she whispered gently. "I will sit here and watch . . ."

Ning took a deep breath and picked up his brush. Miraculously, ideas began to flow again. He lost track of time. She unobtrusively kept his ink fresh, a clean brush close at hand, and a new candle ready. Ning worked through the night. When the first rays of sunlight touched his window, he laid down his brush, expecting to find her curled up under his quilt on the other side of the kang. Instead, the tea kettle spewing steam was the only sign that someone else had been in the room.

Ning's life took a new turn. Day became night. During the day, he slept the dreamless sleep of exhaustion. The girl woke him at dusk. There was no need for words between them. Their souls communed in perfect harmony. He wrote till daybreak without noticing when she slipped away.

Finally the thesis was done. Dressed in his best formal gown, his hair done in a scholar's knot on the top of his head, tied with a sober black ribbon, Ning hurried into the city to submit it, confident he would pass. He was also sure he could not live without the girl. On the way back, he stopped at a shop and selected a hairpin fashioned out of mother-of-pearl. Though he knew nothing about her, not even her name, he would propose marriage that very evening.

However, that evening the girl did not appear. Nor for several evenings thereafter. As daylight faded into another dismal night, the fluttering of a butterfly outside his window startled Ning out of his despair.

"Butterflies aren't nocturnal," he thought, but there it was. The butterfly lighted on the edge of the terrace flexing its wings, as if waiting for him. On an impulse, he went outside. However, the moment he drew near it darted away. Ning followed it into the pine grove. The trees grew so close that their branches shut out what was left of the light. Just when he thought he had lost it, the butterfly appeared, almost close enough to touch. Ning plunged after it again, not knowing or caring where he was going, until his forehead struck something cold and hard. He had run into a wall that marked the lower boundary of the garden. The sound of voices came from the other side. Ning groped his way along, for it was completely dark. Finally he came to a gap where part of the wall had fallen down. On the other side was a stand of ancient bamboos between whose leaves and branches he could make out a cobblestoned terrace lit by a dozen lanterns. Two women were seated there, surrounded by pots of yellow and white chrysanthemums that glowed like stars against the dark shrubbery beyond. The younger of the two was dressing the older one's hair.

"What a ruin this face has become!" complained the crone in a high cracked voice, examining herself in a mirror she held in her hand. "Once upon a time I even turned the Emperor's head."

"Be still, Granny," soothed the other, who looked to be in her late thirties. "When I finish you will look the way you used to!"

"I will soon die!" the old crone's voice rose almost to a shriek. Suddenly she seized the other's hand.

"Granny, don't . . ." The younger woman snatched her hand away and hid it behind her back.

"I knew it, Crystal!" cried the old crone. "You are withering too!"

Crystal averted her face.

"When you could have finished him off, you went soft," the crone shrilled. "Now we are doomed! Oh, the incompetence!" The old crone was working herself into a rage. "The ingratitude! After all I lavished upon you!" Her last remark was heavy with contempt.

The woman called Crystal crumpled to her knees, whimpering.

"Fortunately the girl will save us," quavered the crone. Her head drooped onto her breast as if it were too heavy for her scrawny neck to hold up.

A moment later she lifted her head, nostrils quivering. "I think I smell something," she whispered. "Can you smell it?" she demanded.

"Perhaps the child is back," murmured the other.

"That child!" the crone whined, "I shall whip her!" She flayed the air angrily. The effort exhausted her, for she slumped again in her chair.

A light footstep sounded on the flagstones.

"There you are, naughty child," Crystal scolded. "Granny grows restless when you're tardy."

"It's hard to find the right stuff," replied a young girl. Ning could not see the speaker, but he recognized her voice.

"Give it to me quickly!" cried the crone.

Ning caught the click of a lid against a bowl. The crone made gurgling sounds as she drained its contents in one draft.

"Granny, you didn't leave me any," whined Crystal.

"You don't deserve any," the old woman cackled. To the girl she said in a commanding voice, "Hold up the mirror for me." She examined herself, gesturing for the girl to turn the mirror this way and that. "See, some of the lines are fading." She leaned back with a sigh. In an imperious voice, she order the girl to fetch more!

"Yes!" Crystal chimed in, "I must have some too!"

The girl took a step forward, fell on her knees, and pressed her forehead against the ground. Now Ning was sure it was the object of his affections.

"Please don't send me out again," the girl whimpered. "I'm frightened."

"There is nothing to fear," the old crone cooed. "All you have to do is separate the man from his sword. Then!" She snapped her fingers meaningfully and cackled.

"I can't!" wailed the girl, wrapping her arms around the old one's legs.

"Then take the other one," snapped Crystal.

"What other one?" asked the old crone sharply. "Have you been keeping something from me?" Her eyes darted fire as her gaze swept from Crystal to the girl and back again.

Crystal seized the girl by the scruff of her neck. "Look at that face, Granny! She has betrayed us!"

The girl tried to cover her face with her hands, but the woman pried them loose.

"There is another man in the house," cried the woman vehemently, "young and vigorous." She held the girl's face close to the crone's. "She has been hiding him from us because she fancies him!"

Ning bristled with rage. It was all he could do to keep from leaping over the wall and confronting the women.

The old crone's bony fingers cupped the girl's face.

"I see it's true," she murmured disconsolately. She whirled around and struck Crystal across the face. "First, it was you. Now, this one! I am surrounded by traitors!" she cried.

Ning could not bear to watch any more. Blindly he groped his way out of the pine grove. The light in his window made his breath catch. He sprinted across the terrace and flung open the door. She was seated on the kang, her chin propped on her knees. He stood on the threshold unable to move. She chuckled, and ran to him. He lifted her in his arms and carried her back to the kang.

In the languorous hour after love she whispered, "Tomorrow night I will not be with you . . ." Ning started to protest, but she made him listen. "Don't be alone," she said. "Buy some wine and drink with your neighbor." He objected saying he scarcely knew the man and didn't care for his company. She laid a playful fingertip on his lips. "Do it for me. Make him drunk; then take his sword."

"Why, that's stealing!" exclaimed Ning.

She kissed him softly.

"He is an evil sorcerer," she whispered, her lips against his. "The sword will separate us forever."

He clutched her to him fiercely, vowing nothing could take her from him.

"The sword will destroy me," she sobbed. "In time you will understand! Only it will be too late . . ." She pushed herself away from him. Ning's qualms vanished.

"I will do it," he cried, gathering her into his arms.

Ning woke with the sunlight in his eyes. An earring on his pillow told him the passion of the night before was not a dream. He lay back content. Their vows of love hovered like dust motes dancing in the air.

Ning hurried into town. He bought a jar of good wine and some cooked meats to go with it. When he returned with his purchases late in the afternoon, his neighbor's door stood wide.

"I was expecting you," said the stranger from within.

Ning stammered, shifting his weight from one foot to the other.

"You'd better come in," said the stranger grinning at his discomfiture, "before good food and drink go to waste!"

With a sweep of his hand he cleared a space on the kang.

"There! Not very elegant but it will do," he said, deftly lifting the jar of wine from Ning's grasp.

They ate and drank merrily. Ning never allowed the stranger's cup to go empty. His capacity was astounding. As the level of the wine in the jar dropped, their conversation became more rambling.

"Good and evil take on the weight and form we assign them," began the stranger without preamble. Ning was finding it hard to keep up with the stranger's tirade. The room began to curl at the edges, the kang heaved like a boat on a rough sea, and he longed for sleep.

"This sword is the only weapon against an ancient evil I have pursued for a long time," said the stranger.

Ning snapped to at that remark. For the moment, the kang stopped heaving. The stranger had taken the sword off the wall. Now it lay unsheathed and gleaming across its owner's lap. Blearily Ning remembered his errand.

"May I hold it?" Ning asked.

"You may not," the stranger rumbled.

Ning reached for it nevertheless. The stranger seized his wrist.

"Next time I will take your hand off!" warned the stranger.

A quick glance told Ning the man did not make idle threats.

The stranger was launched on another rambling speech when a raven came through the open window and lighted on a beam overhead. The stranger followed its flight without interrupting himself. Only his grip on the sword tightened. Suddenly the room shuddered, scattering remnants of food and wine across the kang. The next shock bowled Ning over. A howling wind roared through the room. Before his astonished eyes the raven grew to an enormous size, eyeing the two men below, emitting clicking sounds. With a wild cry it swooped down upon the stranger, but the smallness of the room and the bunches of herbs festooning it hampered the bird's movements. Its prey easily rolled out of its reach. Ning wedged himself into a corner, scared sober. The stranger slid off the kang, chanting an incantation, sword at the ready. The bird hopped across the floor, its baleful eyes darting from side to side. The distance between the combatants quickly shortened. With a desperate cry the bird lunged, drawing blood. The stranger whirled about, his sword tracing a shining circle around him. The bird attacked again with deadly precision. The stranger stood his ground, fending off the blood-crazed creature with punishing blows. The battle see-sawed, with the advantage shifting from one to the other. Both man and bird were soon drenched in blood.

Reeling with weariness, the stranger hefted his sword with both hands. With a terrifying squeal the bird, dragging an injured wing, hobbled in for the kill. Mustering what strength he had left, the stranger charged. They met head on. The bird let out an almost human scream and fluttered to the ground, impaled on the stranger's sword. For a moment the woman called Crystal lay where the bird had been. A sickening odor of burning flesh filled the air as she crumbled.

Ning was glad to be behind the bolted door of his own room again. He was shaking so hard he could not light the candle, so he sat shivering in the dark. When a hand reached out and touched his, he cried out in terror.

"It's only me," whispered the girl. They clung to each other, muttering incoherent words of comfort.

"The Old One will come to wreak vengeance," the girl trembled. "If you love me, do me one last favor."

"The sword!" Ning whispered in despair.

"It does not matter now," said the girl, struggling from his arms. "The Old One is a witch who has lived for centuries. Those whom she enslaves drain the blood of humans for her to drink. That is how she stays alive. In return she promises her minions eternal youth and beauty. I was vain and foolish, so I became her slave."

Ning cried out for he could not believe what he was hearing. But the girl made him listen.

"I came to kill you that rainy night. Had you allowed me to stay, or accepted the gold I offered you, the Old One would have drunk your blood. But you did not take advantage of me. Your generosity saved you . . ."

Ning shook his head in disbelief.

"A bundle of bones is buried between two elm trees in a clearing in the woods nearby," she continued breathlessly. "That is where I lie. If you love me, take my bones across the river. Give them a decent burial and I shall be free. You will be safe too on the farther shore, as the Old One cannot cross water."

"What about us?" cried Ning. "I want to marry you . . ."

"That cannot be," replied the girl sadly, "for I do not belong in your world."

"Were our vows of love mere illusion?" Ning persisted.

The girl shook her head miserably.

"We will meet again in another time . . . another place . . ."

Ning started to say something, but his voice ricocheted off the walls. He was alone. He crept to the door, opened it a crack. The stranger's window was a square of light. From within came the sound of chanting. Ning ran from the courtyard into the woods.

Ning had no idea where he was going. It was pitch dark. A force stronger than he propelled him. He plunged on, crashing through the underbrush, tripping, falling, picking himself up and continuing, till he came to a clearing where two elms stood. He found a stout stick and began to dig between them. He did not have to dig long before his stick struck something that did not feel like earth. He widened the hole with bare hands. Just as the girl had said, his fingers encountered a bundle of coarse fabric. Carefully he pulled it out of the earth and clutched it to his breast. The instinct or prescience that guided him evaporated. He stood listening to the night sounds not knowing what to do. Over the thundering of his heart, he heard the sound of water and remembered. The river! He tied the amazingly small bundle of bones across one shoulder and plunged headlong in the direction from which the sound came.

The starless night was thick and black. The trees and the underbrush tore at him. Treacherous vines clutched at his ankles. It was as though the woods were trying to hold him fast. Ning's breath came in harsh rasps. The pain in his chest spread like a slow-burning fire, turning his legs to putty. When he could run no more, he scrambled on all fours. Sometimes the sound of the river was on his right, then on his left, but never nearer. He was going around in circles. Overcome by weariness, he fell facedown on the dew-wet ground. All he wanted was to lie there, never to move again. A faint fluttering in the air close to his face made Ning open his eyes. A butterfly hovered inches from his nose, its frantic fluttering seemed to convey something. Ning struggled to his feet. The butterfly flew up, dancing in the air. Too weary to think, Ning let his feet carry him wherever the butterfly led, pushing himself through the blackness, arms churning the air like a windmill. As suddenly as it had appeared the butterfly vanished, but he could feel moisture in the air, and the rush of water was loud in his ears. He had found the river.

The sky was turning a deep indigo. The night was almost over. In the faint light the river did not seem wide, but the current was swift. He could just make out the slick, wet stones of a ford going across.

He started toward it, each step making a sucking sound as he sank into thick, clinging mud. Suddenly an old woman's voice called from the dark woods behind.

"Young man, I am lost. Won't you please give me a hand?"

Ning gritted his teeth and pressed on. The mud made every step an effort.

"Young man," the old woman's voice was full of pleading, "I will perish!"

Ning's heart was lodged in his throat. He dared not stop, for with every step he sank a little deeper.

"Young man, I am utterly alone," cried the old woman, "Help me!"

With a loud splash Ning fell forward into the river. The old woman on the bank let loose a fearful howl of rage. The trees thrashed. The rocks trembled. The river, churning with fury, dragged him under.

Twice Ning bobbed to the surface, gasping for air, and twice he was sucked under again. The river was carrying him back to shore.

"Give me what is mine," the old woman laughed triumphantly, "or you die!"

"Never!" cried Ning as another wave pulled him under.

The next time he came to the surface, Ning was thrown against a half-submerged rock. Though the river continued to buffet him, he wrapped his arms around it as tight as he could, and the rock held him up. The old crone was out of breath. As her howling subsided, the woods gradually became still, and the river calmed. Leaning heavily on her cane the old crone tottered toward where the reeds grew. Instantly her cane became stuck in the mud. She grasped it with both hands trying to free it, but the mud would not let go. The more she worried it, the tighter it held. She lost her footing and slid into the mud. Her shrieks set the river churning again, but only for an instant. The old crone had sunk knee deep in mud. Though her mouth opened and shut, not another sound came out of her.

There was a sudden movement. The stranger emerged from the dark, his sword flashing ominously. The old crone hissed and spat, clawed the air like an angry cat, but she was stuck fast.

Ning let go of the rock, and struck out for the farther shore.

The old crone let out a despairing howl. There was a flash of light followed by a loud crack. When Ning looked back from across the river, the stranger stood wearily clutching the bladeless hilt of his sword. All that was left of the old crone was a tattered robe floating slowly down stream. The stranger raised his hand in farewell and disappeared into the woods.

Weeks later, Ning arrived home, having first buried the bundle of bones he had carried all that way in a corner of an orchard nearby. His father pulled a long face, convinced Ning's tattered and dirty condition meant he had failed again.

"At least you're none the worse for wear," growled the old man.

Months later, just when the father was about to press him into joining the family business, Ning was notified that he had not only passed the Imperial Civil Service Examination but he had been appointed magistrate of his hometown, replacing the incumbent, who was too old to preside over the court.

Ning became renowned for the wisdom and fairness of his judgments. While the father had ample reason to be proud of his achievements, he was chagrined by Ning's refusal to marry. Years later Ning bought the orchard, to which he had become attached. He planted two elms in a corner and placed two stone benches in their shade. It became his retreat, where he went to read and meditate. When he died, he was buried there according to his wishes. It is said that two butterflies appeared, danced a while over the new grave, then disappeared into the sunlight.